THE
Spirit
Challenge

ROBERT WILSON &
SR. MARIE McARDLE

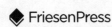 FriesenPress

Suite 300 - 990 Fort St
Victoria, BC, V8V 3K2
Canada

www.friesenpress.com

ISBN
978-1-5255-0667-3 (Hardcover)
978-1-5255-0668-0 (Paperback)
978-1-5255-0669-7 (eBook)

1. Body, Mind & Spirit, Healing, Prayer & Spiritual

Distributed to the trade by The Ingram Book Company

As a people,
we've forgotten
who we are.

CONTENTS

ACKNOWLEDGEMENTS

This body of work could not have been conceived or produced without the guidance and promptings of the Holy Spirit.

Once the initial concept crystalized, it became clear that the path to completion would require an earthly alter ego.

To this end, I sought out my friend in faith, Sister Marie McArdle to collaborate on this project.

Marie has tirelessly given of herself, with much care, and assisted in the formation, logistics, and co-writing of what you are about to read. For this, I am eternally grateful.

The editing stage was patiently and thoughtfully conducted by Tony Myres.

Able contributors to a selected number of photographs found herein include my daughter Mary Lynn and son Jeffrey.

To all of these, not the least of whom is my wife Margaret, who lovingly contributed her time, patience, and understanding, I bow in thankful humility and spiritual attachment.

Robert Wilson
(co-author)

PREFACE

We are all born of the flesh—born of the spirit. Our life becomes a battle of priorities between the flesh and the spirit.

Each one of us is so pre-occupied with placing emphasis on the external events of our lives that we allow our internal self to slowly deteriorate.

We have the ability to bring a peaceful resolve to all conflicts that exist, whether simmering at a world-wide level or unfolding in front of our very eyes. The outer world, the arena of action and engagement, is the battlefield. Our inner self (the very spirit of who we are) is made up of a spirit of love, peace, and brotherhood. It is where we go for answers. It is our island of sanity and the place where the spirit lives.

Our spirit is continually challenged by outside forces.

DEDICATION

*That the efforts of mankind to make the world more
human be purified and strengthened by the power of God
and the individual spirit, working hand in hand.
Oh, the awe and wonder of it all!*

"In contact with the beauties of the mountains,
in the face of the spectacular grandeur of the peaks,
the fields of snow and the immense landscapes,
man enters into himself and discovers
that the beauty of the universe shines
not only in the framework of
the exterior heavens, but also,
that of the soul that allows itself
to be enlightened, and that seeks
to give meaning to life."

— Pope John Paul II

AUTHOR'S NOTE

What you are about to read is made up of a lifelong gathering of thoughts, observations, and conclusions from the mind of a member of the human race. I have interlaced these words with quotes from a number of different sources, not the least of which is Christian Scripture.

The body and soul age differently in every person. In my case, at seventy-five years of age (the winter of my years), my body is slowly deteriorating, and yet my soul seems to be expanding and thriving through acquired knowledge that is slowly fermenting into wisdom.

Two examples of this are my lifelong tendency to grapple with the face of a problem or to search for an answer within the limits of the perceived darkness of the predicament. What I have learned is that what you cannot see can be seen from a different part of the mountain. I refer to the mountain of spiritual enlightenment. It is my belief that if we allow it to happen, the Holy Spirit will direct and lead us to the top of the mountain.

As we gaze upon the billowy puff of clouds in the sky, as we breathe in the pure air, and almost reach out to the peaks of the mountain, we have before us a cathedral in the highlands, a creation of God, the Father Almighty.

I share with you a prayer that invites the Holy Spirit to attend to your very spirit.

An Anxious Person's Prayer

— William Browning, CP

O Holy Spirit, give me stillness of soul in you.
Calm the turmoil within with the gentleness of your peace.
Quiet the anxiety within with a deep trust in you.
Heal the wounds of sin within
with the joy of your forgiveness.
Strengthen the faith within
with the awareness of your presence.
Confirm the hope within
With the knowledge of your strength.
Give fullness to the love within
with an outpouring of your love.
O Holy Spirit, be to me a source of light,
strength and courage
so that I may hear your call ever more clearly
and follow you more generously.
Amen

The second example is related to some health issues in my life (we all have them). The road of ill health can be one of slow and painful recovery. What I have come to realize is that we are not alone on this path and that our pain, anxiety, and fear can be shared. My mantra during these times is "give the pain to God."

Pathway of Pain

—Helen Steiner Rice

If my days were untroubled and my heart always light,
Would I seek that fair land where there is no night?
If I never grew weary with the weight of my load,
would I search for God's peace at the end of the road?

If I never knew sickness and never knew pain,
would I search for a hand to help and sustain?
If I walked not with sorrow and lived without loss,
would my soul seek sweet solace at the foot of the cross?

If all I desired was mine day by day,
would I kneel before God and earnestly pray?
If God sent no 'winter' to freeze me with fear,
would I yearn for the warmth of 'spring' every year?

I ask myself this and the answer is plain.
If my life were all pleasure and I never knew pain
I'd seek God less often and need Him much less,
for God's sought more often in times of distress.

And no one knows God or sees Him as plain,
as those who have met Him on the "Pathway of Pain."

These are but two examples of giving you a life within the spirit. The challenges of life are many, and the simple message is that we are not alone.

CHAPTER 1

LIFE WITHIN THE SPIRIT

We are all children of God! We are all born of a sinful nature! These two facts are part of our evolution in life, and as we progress to the age of reason, our choices are made from a combination of the spirit within us (the child of God's creation) and from our sinful nature which is nourished by the external world (all that glitters is not gold) outside of us.

Why during our lifetime do we have a tendency to be drawn to the magnet of that exterior world? A better question would be: why do we not first consult with or meditate on what direction our very spirit is taking us?

Life By The Spirit

"My counsel is this: Live freely, animated and motivated by God's Spirit. Then you won't feed the compulsions of selfishness. For there is a root of sinful self-interest in us that is at odds with a free spirit, just as the free spirit is incompatible with selfishness. .... Why don't you choose to be led by the Spirit? .... It is obvious what kind of life- time: repetitive, loveless, cheap sex; a stinking accumulation of mental and emotional garbage; frenzied and joyless grabs for happiness; . . . I could go on. If you use your freedom this way, you will not inherit God's kingdom. But what happens when we live God's way? He brings gifts into our lives, things like affection for others, exuberance about life, serenity ... Among those who belong to Christ, everything connected with getting our own way and mindlessly responding to what everyone else calls necessities is killed off for good. Since this is the kind of life we have chosen, the life of the Spirit, let us make sure that we do not just hold it as an idea in our heads or a sentiment in our hearts, but work out its implications in every detail of our lives. That means we will not compare ourselves with each other as if one of us were better and another worse. We have far more interesting things to do with our lives. Each of us is an original!"
(Galatians 5:16–25 MSG)

Those who belong to Christ Jesus attempt to crucify their sinful nature with its passions and desires. Since we live by the Spirit, let us keep in step with the Spirit. Day by day, we work at trying to be the best person we can be! The obstructions are endless. We keep trying. The singer Peggy Lee sings, "Is that all there is?" As we look to seek out the answer to this question, the importance of attempting to break through these obstructions becomes the challenge. The question becomes, "Where does the truth begin and just where do we place our values?" The answer can be found in the personal decision to turn away from all that represents external thinking, the wall that prevents us from getting in touch with our internal selves (which is where the Holy Spirit is found).

At one point, Jesus turns to his Apostles and says, "In a few days, you will be baptized by the Holy Spirit" (Acts 1:5 MSG).

This release of the Holy Spirit in our life is the "Promise of the Father", that Jesus made possible for us when he died, rose, and ascended (Acts 1:4 MSG).

The Holy Spirit is a positive gift to us from God, which helps us to understand the love and truth that exist between God, the Father, and the Son, Jesus Christ. This gift is there for us to call upon, to rely on, and use all the days of our lives. This gift of the Holy Spirit is always available, always, and is truly a treasure, as it enables us to make a positive distinction between the darkness that can pervade our lives and the light that leads us to love and truth. In the free will that God has given us, the choice is always ours.

The long road home

Sometimes, we walk through this external life with a singular or solitary feeling of being alone. Nothing could be further from the truth.

The following chapter is a compilation of thoughts and scripture verses, which form a message to us that speaks volumes in terms of our walking this path of life, never afraid, never alone.

CHAPTER 2

MY BELOVED

Do not be fooled by the evil one. He will try to convince you that you have wandered too far from God and you cannot come back. That is never true. God is compassionate and gracious, slow to anger, and abounding in love. If you confess your sins, God will be faithful and just and will forgive your sins and purify you from all unrighteousness.

> *"If your heart is broken, you'll find God right there;*
> *if you're kicked in the gut, he'll help you catch your breath".*
> *(Psalms 34:18 MSG)*

Have you ever wondered how high the heavens reach? God's love for you is higher than that. And how far do you think the east is from the west? That is how far God has removed your sins from you. When you ask for forgiveness, they are gone. So, do not go looking for them; do not even try to remember them, because God does not.

Be glad when you come before God. He loves to hear you sing joyful songs of praise. Just think of all the benefits you enjoy as God's child. And as you rejoice and give thanks to Him even in difficult times, He will fill you with a peace that you cannot explain.

So, do not listen to the evil one anymore. He only wants to rob you of your joy, the joy you will find in God's presence. Approach God's throne of grace with confidence, and you will receive mercy and find grace to help you in your time of need. Come, even now, for God is waiting for you.

Read the following scripture passages and discover how much God loves you!

> *Psalm 16:11; 100:2, 103:5–8,11–12;*
> *Philippians 4:4–7, & Hebrews 10:17*

Many of my personal experiences have helped me turn away from the evil one and come closer to my loving God. At one point in my life, I recognized that my lifestyle was being dominated by a social whirlwind that included a reliance on alcohol, as well as a set of priorities that were, for the most part, meaningless.

I recall driving along a highway in the dead of night, and as I gazed out at the stretch of road ahead of me, I found myself talking to God, asking, and praying for an answer to my questions, "Where is this road of life taking me? What are the building blocks of my life? Do I have a mission yet unaccomplished?"

As I continued to ponder these questions, I started to pray and through prayer found myself reflecting on the roots of my Christian upbringing and my loss of those values. I also began to realize I had been given certain gifts to use in this life and was not using them. I had my health, an inventive mind, time at my disposal, and a fairly good way with people. I prayed, and as I prayed, the question arose in my mind, "What would Jesus do?"

I believe the Holy Spirit answered my prayers that night because, in the midst of my chosen words, I found myself saying "Lord, let me find my peace on this earth by representing you, by being a beacon for you here on earth, and carrying out your work, your Holy Will." It became a plan, it remained to simply execute the details and make a reality of my new-found mission.

The details of that plan began to unfold in myriad ways. For the next few days, I looked around my community, seeking out a need or an area where a difference could be made. In a short time, I was made aware of the need for a breakfast program in the nearby rural grade school. I along with five parishioners in our local parish, instituted a fund-raising program (soliciting used household items and clothing for resale in the basement of the Church) that allowed us to buy ingredients to feed approximately 30 children. Once a month, we gathered in the basement of the church where there was a kitchen, and baked muffins and prepared juice for distribution.

My inward prayers had resulted in an outward action, which was helpful to someone else, and gratifying to my newfound mission. God had answered my prayer!

Within each of us is the Spirit of cultivating the land.

In reaching out and developing a communication with the Lord, by asking for a remedy to my problem, I was able to remedy someone else's problem. Thank you, Lord, for helping me find my way. Please help me to continue to help others who have lost their direction to look inward, to the part of their being that is the spirit of self, combined with the Holy Spirit of God, a combination that cannot be defeated.

There is a message in this little story, and that message is that we all have the opportunity to open up a dialogue with God, our Creator. With that dialogue of prayer, we open the floodgates of love, and that dialogue of love is then passed on to our fellow man through a journey of love, which began with the Cross, the Passion of Christ, and on to a risen life, which is promised to all of us. God, our Creator, wants us to move into the future with Him. It all begins with the dialogue of love and prayer.

> *"Love the Lord your God with all your passion*
> *and prayer and intelligence ..."*
> *(Matthew 22:37 MSG)*

CHAPTER 3

WE DO HAVE A CHOICE!

Although God's love is always with us, we cannot forget that human freedom is limitless! We have forgotten that God has created each of us with our own spirit and free will. Within each of us is the Holy Spirit of God, who is waiting for us to ask that the knots of our human affairs be loosened and untangled.

We were conceived in the heart of God and for this reason,

> "*Each of us is the result of a thought of God, each of us is willed, each of us is loved, each of us is necessary.*"

— Pope Benedict XVI

> "*Before I formed you in the womb, I knew you.*"
> (*Jeremiah 1:5 MSG*)

The love and strength of God is our joy. How are we to make it our centrepiece? With all our worldly problems, how do we find God's joy in their midst? We need to put our troubles in perspective and remember that everyone, without exception, experiences trials of some sort. God has a purpose even in our troubles, to form us, to teach us, to help us grow. We can experience the joy of the Lord by knowing that God loves us. He is with us, even in troublesome times, and He will bring us through the difficulties we are facing.

We need to put God first in our lives. The acrostic F.I.R.S.T. spells out for us some of the things we must do if we are to put God in the center of our lives.

F stands for focus.

We need to take time, to pray, to focus on God's unconditional love for us, to receive the Sacrament of the Eucharist so we can be bread for others.

I stands for identify.

We need to identify the gifts God has given us so we may use them for the poor, lonely, sick, weak, and imprisoned.

R stands for respect.

Jesus prayed Our Father (ABBA) meaning our Daddy. We need to respect God's majesty and remember that we are all children of God.

S stands for service.

Jesus came to serve, not to be served. He asked us to feed the hungry, give drink to the thirsty, shelter the homeless...

T stands for teaching others.

Saint Francis tells us, "Preach the Gospel at all times. Use words if necessary!" This simply means that our actions at work, home, and in the community should be such that others will know we love God.

On a personal level, we all face anxieties of both mental strain and physical pain. Normally we turn to a professional for assistance. This is an obvious external action that has the potential of a materialistic solution. What about the soothing of our spirit?

Turning inward to focus on the voice within us, the Holy Spirit of love and truth becomes the doctor of our soul. In this way, a relationship is formed between the individual (soul) and the Holy Spirit, which is nurtured and thrives on the gift of faith.

Praise and worship through the power of prayer soothe our spirit.

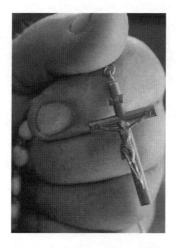

"Saying one's prayers isn't exactly the same thing as praying."
L. M. Montgomery, *Anne of Green Gables*

Some of us have lost the ability to pray. We read words, we say words, but there is no deep meaning. We search for a way to unscramble our thoughts and to put form to our communicative prayer.

Is it possible that we have lost touch with the one who has created us? How can we give meaning to our prayer? The answer is quite simple. It is to begin with inner peace, an interior peace that can only be achieved by establishing a relationship with God that is unencumbered by the meaningless clutter, that is, too often, at the forefront of our minds. We prioritize the events, problems, and complexities of our lives, and as they increase, our ability to go to our island of peace is diminished and put on the back burner.

Prayer is talking to God. St. Teresa of Avila sums up prayer by saying, "Prayer is nothing else but being on friendly terms of friendship with God." Just as we tell our friends our plans, our difficulties, and our joys and sorrows, so too we can share all of this with our Best Friend, God.

Prayer, however, is not just dumping all our fears, mistakes on God and then walking away. We must also listen to what our friend God is saying to us.

Prayer does not just happen when we go to church or kneel at our bedside. A story a friend told me clarifies this. She wrote to her Spiritual Director, who was a Jesuit priest, to tell him she did not have time to pray, because she taught all day and then was the chauffeur for the sisters who lived in the convent with her, for they could not drive. Her Spiritual Director wrote her back and said, "You are deaf, blind and dumb! Why are you not praying in the car as you wait for the sister to finish her errand?" My friend laughed as she said she never thought of praying in the car. We can pray in the car, in the shopping centre, at work, if we say, "Jesus I offer this out of love for you."

CHAPTER 4

EQUALITY

Our journey, with God as our centre, means we must begin with the premise that we are all created equal. We are all creations of a supreme being, God! This creation of God is in the form of a mould, made up of the body (physical), mind (intellect), and spirit (soul).

As creatures created separate from the animal kingdom, we are given intellectual capacity. We also differ from the animal kingdom in that we have an inner spirit that is part of our created selves. However, this inner self is all too often ignored and seldom nurtured.

The animal kingdom is unique.

The history of man as we know it, in both oral and written form, leaves us with facts rampant in the physical and intellectual sphere. Hardly ever does oral or written history dwell on our spiritual heritage. One could argue that the Bible and its scriptural readings and passages make up for this lack of spiritual heritage. This argument is true, except that many generations of us have confused our spiritual heritage with a word that unfortunately has, in my opinion, detracted from our inner spiritual presence, or resolve. That word is "religion."

Too many of us confuse our spiritual being with some form or type of religion that for the most part, is to be traced to the origin of man.

The Word of God originates as an inspiration of the Holy Spirit, having been translated from the inspired Word of God, which becomes the basis of faith. Unfortunately, man has gone beyond the Holy Spirit's promptings and teachings, with interpretations that have resulted in different faith beliefs or sects. These different faith beliefs or sects have been categorized under the umbrella of religion.

For the purposes of clarity and understanding, the author has a belief system that is based on the Christian tradition that follows the universal faith, Roman Catholicism. This belief system follows the scriptural readings of the life of Jesus Christ.

All of our faith beliefs are the central part of our spirit and should not be confused with the scattered world of organized religion. We have allowed ourselves to become adversaries over this word religion.

Recently, I spoke with an acquaintance who described himself as a humanist when asked if he was a Christian. In explaining, he said: "Too many wars in history have been fought over religion."

Somehow, we must use our individual belief systems to move forward in nurturing our spirits. Each of us must draw upon our interior promptings, in forging the day-to-day decisions we make and not be led or swayed by the negative external noise around us.

God, our Father, gave Christ Jesus the Son an eternal purpose and that purpose is reflected in EVERY child of God on this earth.

Our spirituality is not made up of splintered facts. Our spirituality is made up of the relationship we work at on a daily basis, and that relationship is with God, our Creator.

The sum total of God, our Creator, is found in the spirit of the Trinity, Father, Son, and Holy Spirit. That Spirit lies within each one of us through faith in Him.

> "My response is to get down on my knees before the Father, this magnificent Father who parcels out all heaven and earth. I ask Him to strengthen you by His Spirit—not a brute strength but a glorious inner strength—that Christ will live in you as you open the door and invite Him in. And I ask Him that with both feet planted firmly on love, you'll be able to take in with all followers of Jesus the extravagant dimensions of Christ's love. Reach out and experience the breadth! Test its length! Plumb the depths! Rise to the heights! Live full lives, full in the fullness of God." (Ephesians 3:14–19 MSG)

If there is an equality to be found in the human family (the world around us), then there must also be unity. How can there be unity without love and understanding? It is with this very love and understanding that relationships are forged.

Hope

We must avoid making unfair judgements and never use derogatory expressions or actions that would make dialogue and mutual cooperation untenable. We need to be open to deep conversion of heart, to pray for the humility and offer our lives in the service of others. We must also pray for forgiveness for the sins against unity we have made and continue to make.

As children of God, unity becomes a key strength in our relations with others. Unity is built on trust, on forgiveness, on love, on understanding, and on respect. In our hurry-up world, we sometimes lose touch with treating others in the manner we would like to be treated. The following true story is an example of many situations we all find ourselves in as we walk down the pathways of our lives.

At one point in my life, I was asked to act as administrator of the parish I was assigned to as a deacon. There was a need for a bookkeeper in the parish. For various reasons, a suitable or qualified person could not be found within the congregation. After advertising for this position in the weekly bulletin, I was made aware of a woman who lived in the area but was not a parishioner, nor was she attending a Church on a regular basis. I called her in for an interview and found her to be qualified and affordable. Upon recommendation to the Pastor of the parish, she was hired on a part-time basis, to assist us with the parish's bookkeeping.

Shortly after this, a leading member of the parish took me aside, questioning and complaining about the decision to hire this particular woman in this position. Her initial concern did not centre around a lack of qualification. It centered around an incident or incidents that had transpired as the two of them were growing up, some fifteen or twenty years earlier. As I attempted to explain that these facts were possibly no longer pertinent or relevant, she said, "How could you hire her here at the Church, she doesn't attend Mass on Sunday or go to church at all." I explained that this was not necessarily a criterion for completing the work that needed to be accomplished in this position. This explanation did not appease her. The footnote to this story is that a small network of similar complaints trickled in.

People were concerned that a mistake had been made in filling this position with a non-member of the congregation. The ironic part of the story is that this newly hired woman went on not only to do an admirable job with the bookkeeping of the parish, but she also began attending Mass on a regular basis and has returned to the faith that she had allowed to slip.

Why is it that we sometimes cannot accept, attempt to understand, respect, or forgive one another? How can we achieve any kind of unity when we base our thoughts on prejudice, lack of forgiveness, or make judgements that are not for us to make, but for God to make? We must allow the "door to our hearts" be opened and allow the Holy Spirit to advise, to nurture, and to heal.

CHAPTER 5

WHO AM I?

The journey of our soul has an influence and impact on those around us. Everyone that walks the face of this earth is a unique creation of God! No two persons are exactly the same. We all have different body types, different complexities of mind, and each of us has a distinct and incomparable spirit that ultimately forms the substance and character of who we are.

The challenge is to determine the essence of our individual being and discover, who am I? When we were created by God, the picture that was painted or the form that was sculpted became very personal, as it was created by a God that was working from a canvas of love. Into the mix, there were many elements, not the least of which was our family genes, which mixed with the God-given gifts that would come to constitute the person that God had created.

> *"What you are is God's gift to you,*
> *what you become is your gift to God."*

— Hans Urs von Balthasar

To fulfill the high calling that God has placed upon you in creating you, and redeeming you, you must come to grips with who you really are, inside and out, for you *will* do what you are.

"What marvelous love the Father has extended to us! Just look at it—we're called children of God! That's who we really are. But that's also why the world doesn't recognize us or take us seriously, because it has no idea who He is or what He's up to. But friends, that's exactly who we are: children of God. And that's only the beginning. Who knows how we'll end up! What we know is that when Christ is openly revealed, we'll see Him—and in seeing Him, become like Him. All of us who look forward to his coming stay ready, with the glistening purity of Jesus' life as a model for our own."
(1 John 3 MSG)

Speedy Muffler has an advertisement that says "You're a Somebody." Most of us, I believe, reject this idea, for we often compare ourselves to successful others or with those we consider important. However, Jesus tells us we are more than a "Somebody": we are children of God.

What does this mean? Well, first we were created by an artist who is greater than Michelangelo. We know most of us could never afford to buy a sculpture done by this great artist nor would we deface this art in any way. Our creator God is greater than any famous artist. This makes us too expensive, too valuable, to consider ourselves not good enough or not important. Secondly, God, our creator, loved us so much He sent His son Jesus to die for us. He did this so we would have the gift of eternal life. How loved we are! Thirdly, since we are heirs to God's kingdom, we are God's princes and God's princesses.

As we venture forth into life, we are influenced by our parents, relatives, teachers, friends, and associates. Through this web of contacts, we gravitate towards a maturity and understanding that leads to relationships that can be bonding or casual as our choices and free will dictate. Our choices vary from individual to individual and can be as intricate as surrendering to God or as simple as choosing a mate (soul mate), close friend, or mentor with whom to hopefully build a trusting and lasting relationship.

Throughout this journey, each soul interacts with another in a meaningful way. There is always an influence, a mark, a trail resulting in the lessons we learn as a result of our encounters. Along this path, we sometimes lose touch with the fact, that the canvas of love that was first created by God, is one of free will, which allows us to be our own person and at the same time be aware of the path that was originally designed by God.

Commenting on the gift of free will, the Greek philosopher Heraclitus wrote,

> "The content of your character is your choice.
> Day by day, what you choose, what you think,
> and what you do is who you become."

The daily decisions, the choices we make on how we conduct and live out our lives, are unique and personal, our very own. Even in the most difficult of circumstances, we DO have a choice as to how we react. So, in the final analysis, it is up to us whether we are happy or unhappy in this world. We will act according to the perception of who we truly are, whether these perceptions are accurate or not.

One of our deepest fears is that of not being good enough. Of not being smart enough, attractive enough, loveable enough, strong enough, motivated enough, or enough in any other capacity. These feelings stem from a vision of what we "should" be, rather than loving and embracing exactly who we are.

In God's eyes, you are enough. Even if others judge your past, your abilities or any other human qualities, God loves you exactly the way you are. Give up your fears, and know that God isn't looking for perfection from you, He just looks at you struggling each day to please Him. Rejoice each day in the gifts that He has given. Every day strive to be the best that you can be during your time here on earth.

There is a child within all of us.

Don't forget to rejoice in exactly who you are. Be confident in your gifts and the knowledge that YOU ARE ENOUGH.

CHAPTER 6

WHAT IS GOD'S PURPOSE FOR US?

If we look in the early manuals of instruction in the principles of the Christian religion, we find help in becoming the best person we can be in a question and answer format, of why God made us. We are told that God made us (a) to know Him, (b) to love Him, and (c) to serve Him in this world, and be happy with Him forever in Heaven.

To know Him!

Jesus described God as an Abba (a loving Daddy). This word for "father" comes from Aramaic, a language spoken in Palestine at the time of Jesus; Abba was a term used by children in addressing their fathers. Jesus used Abba to express his relationship with God and taught his disciples to pray to God as a loving and loveable parent.

Most of us would describe God as a judge, who watches with His big eye to see if we've kept all the rules and commandments He gave us. Although describing God as Abba can cause pain to those whose earthly Fathers have treated them badly, Abba here refers to a Dad who loves, protects, and cares. So, do you know God? Is He an Abba daddy for you?

To love Him!

Within each of us is the spirit of coming home

"God loves you. He loved you yesterday.
He loves you tomorrow.
He loves you always regardless if you mess up."
(Hebrews 13:8 MSG)

Matthew's Gospel tells us that we are to love God with our whole mind and heart. Jesus said:

"Love the Lord your God with all of your passion and
prayer and intelligence. This is most important, the first
on any list. But there is a second to set alongside it:
"Love others as well as you love as you love yourself."
(Matthew 22:37–39 MSG)

Imagine for a moment someone you really love and admire. Don't you want to be near that person often? Do you find yourself wanting to imitate this person? Well, that's how we are to love God. However, if you want this kind of relationship, you must spend time with Him. You need to talk to Him, imitate Him, thank Him, bring Him all your questions and doubts. We must also listen to Him by reading the scriptures to discover what He wants us to do. Then we need to surrender all our worldly desires so we can give all our attention to Him.

To serve Him!

> Then he said, "Do you understand what I have done to
> you? You address me as 'Teacher' and 'Master,' and rightly
> so. That is what I am. So, if I, the Master and Teacher,
> washed your feet, you must now wash each other's feet.
> I've laid down a pattern for you. What I've done, you do.
> I'm only pointing out the obvious. A servant is not ranked
> above his master; an employee doesn't give orders to the
> employer. If you understand what I'm telling you,
> act like it—and live a blessed life."
> (John 13:12–17 MSG)

So, you are saying to yourself, what does God want me to do? To discover this, we need to look at our spiritual gifts, heart, abilities, personality, and experiences. Let's look at what it takes to learn to serve like Jesus. First Jesus made Himself available to the sick, the poor, and the outcast. He stopped along His journey to speak and heal them. Today, our business, self-centeredness, perfectionism, and materialism keep us from dropping everything to serve our neighbour. If we really want to have a servant heart, like Jesus Christ, we won't mind being interrupted every time we meet someone in need, for it will be our opportunity to lend a helping hand like Jesus did.

In Paul's letter to the Galatians, he says:

> *"Live creatively, friends. If someone falls into sin,*
> *forgivingly restore him, saving your critical comments for*
> *yourself. You might be needing forgiveness before the day's*
> *out. Stoop down and reach out to those who are oppressed.*
> *Share their burdens, and so complete Christ's law. If you*
> *think you are too good for that, you are badly deceived.*
>
> *Make a careful exploration of who you are and the work*
> *you have been given, and then sink yourself into that.*
> *Don't be impressed with yourself.*
> *Don't compare yourself with others"*
> *(Galatians 6:1–5 MSG)*

It will be in these small services that we grow like Christ. Jesus specialized in menial tasks that everyone else tried to avoid: washing feet, helping children, fixing breakfast, and serving lepers. Small tasks often show a big heart. Your servant's heart is revealed in little acts that others don't think of doing. No task is beneath you when you have a servant's heart.

To be happy with Him forever in Heaven!

One day, you're going to stand before God, and He's going to say to you, "What did you do with what I gave you, the talents, the abilities, the background, the experiences, the freedom, the education, and the family experiences?"

CHAPTER 7

CONFLICT AND PAIN

Knowing, loving, and serving God, however, will not give us Heaven on earth. We will experience conflict and pain. The definition of a conflict is a fight or disagreement. Conflict means to clash with someone or something. Conflict occurs when I want A, and you want B, and I think that if you get B, I can't have A, so I compete to get what I want.

Conflict is about justice and wrongdoing, and it is a part of being human. In times of conflict, one's true self is shown. Conflict is a natural element in the world and is a part of our everyday lives. A possible solution to the struggles or encounters we are having with other people is to approach the person you are having the disagreement with, offering a well-thought-out and intelligent comprehension of how you view both sides of the issue. This particular state of mind is best reached through a window of humility. The challenge is to resolve with peace in your heart and dialogue as your goal. Where there is a spirit of hostility, let, a spirit of thoughtful dialogue take its place. This can be accomplished applying a spirit of understanding the culture of the differences that exist.

The goal in any dialogue should be to achieve unity, not victory. Constructive dialogue should be focussed more on listening, more than talking, trading ideas, and coming to a deeper and more rational understanding. Dialogue is based on the belief that when people have the feeling they are being listened to and understood, they, in turn, become more willing to listen and the end result is that new possibilities present themselves.

Through the perseverance of dialogue, coupled with the inner strength of prayer, a resolution or remedy is always found. A spirit of understanding and well-thought-out dialogue will trump a spirit of ill will on every occasion.

A letter from James 4:1–3 MSG tells us why conflict happens. He says:

> *"Where do you think all these appalling wars and quarrels come from? Do you think they just happen? Think again. They come about because you want your own way, and fight for it deep inside yourselves. You lust for what you don't have and are willing to kill to get it. You want what isn't yours and will risk violence to get your hands on it. You wouldn't think of just asking God for it, would you? And why not? Because you know you'd be asking for what you have no right to. You're spoiled children, each wanting your own way."*

As Christians, then, can we expect to live a life of holiness without conflict? The answer, of course, is NO! We are continually confronted with a changing society based on a set of values that vary from group to group, and from person to person. We have cultural differences, religious differences, political differences, etc., and the challenge to these differences is ever-present. How to cope? We all have a spirit of being inviting, welcoming, embracing, and affirming. It is to advance and share this positive energy. This quality is most effective when we allow ourselves to first withdraw and learn. In other words, the withdrawal becomes an attempt to get to the bottom of both sides of the conflict, and the learning is gained from listening.

First, withdraw and learn, and then advance and share!

My wife and I now resolve our major disagreements with dialogue that begins with "Let me think about it." Then each of us takes a period of time to digest and form our thoughts. We go to a quiet place in our minds, both in a physical sense and a meditative sense.

We need now to look at how Jesus confronted these conflicts so we will know how to confront ours. First, *Jesus was loving and patient with everyone, even when being personally attacked.* While the religious leaders were openly hostile, Jesus did not respond in anger. He remained calm, focussed, and unaffected by the negativity around him. *To get to the* heart of a matter, *Jesus either reframed their questions or answered using another question.* He challenged people's assumptions and forced them to rethink their attitudes. Jesus showed patience and mercy to all parties. Throughout scripture, Jesus is found to retreat to a quiet place in both prayer and meditation.

Here we can see that we really need to pray for the gifts of the Holy Spirit so we can remain calm, not angry. We need the courage of the Holy Spirit to meet the person challenging us face to face. Gossiping and explaining your side of the conflict to everyone you meet is not of God, and the conflict is not resolved. The pain that arises from the ashes of conflict can sometimes be over-burdening, and if we allow the process to take hold, it can be smothering to our spirit. The trick is to utilize the lessons learned from the experience. The great statesman and historian, Winston Churchill once said: "From the debris of despair, we build our characters." We need to pray for the gifts of the Holy Spirit to resolve conflict, not the least of which is patience and forgiveness!

St. Paul's letter to the Ephesians 4:1–6 MSG says:

> *"As a prisoner for the Lord, then, I urge you to live a life worthy of the calling you have received. Be completely humble and gentle; be patient, bearing with one another in love. Make every effort to keep the unity of the Spirit through the bond of peace. There is one body and one Spirit --- just as you were called to one hope when you were called—one Lord, one faith one baptism, one God and Father who is over all and through all and in all."*

There is an amazing story of reconciliation told by Corrie ten Boom in her book, *The Hiding Place*. Corrie and her family, during World War II, had been imprisoned by the Nazis for giving help to the Jews. Corrie's sister, Betsie, died after being beaten to death by an SS guard.

When Corrie got out of prison, she travelled the world, speaking of God's love. One night, at a church service in Munich, she saw the SS guard who had killed her sister. After the service, he came up to Corrie and said, "I am very grateful for your message of Jesus forgiveness and love." Then he thrust out his hand for her to shake. Corrie's hand remained at her side.

As anger and thoughts of revenge raged through her, she realized that, yes, Jesus died for this man too, and who was she to do less. She prayed, "Forgive me and help me forgive him." Then she took his hand, and as she did a shock went through her arm to him, and at the same time, she felt great love for him. She went on to say, only God can give you the desire and ability to truly forgive others. In God, you will find the courage and the strength you need, to give others the gift of forgiveness and reconciliation.

CHAPTER 8

FORGIVENESS & MERCY

Conflict brings with it the greatest challenge we will ever meet

When we have been hurt, betrayed, undermined, wronged over and over, or rejected, we look for revenge or hold on to a grudge.

> *"Forgiveness is above all a Personal choice.*
> *A decision of the heart*
> *to go against the Natural instinct to*
> *pay back Evil with Evil."*

— John Paul II

However, Jesus told us, "To love your enemies. Let them bring out the best in you, not the worst." (Matthew 5:44 MSG).

To forgive is a conscious, deliberate decision to release feelings of resentment or vengeance towards a person or group who has harmed you, regardless of whether they actually deserve your forgiveness. Forgiveness is *not* glossing over or denying the seriousness of an offence against you. Forgiveness does not mean forgetting, nor does it mean condoning or excusing offences. Though forgiveness can help repair a damaged relationship, it doesn't obligate you to reconcile with the person who harmed you, or release that person from legal accountability.

"The weak can never forgive.
Forgiveness is the attribute of the strong!"

— Mahatma Gandhi

Forgiveness is never easy, so how do we do it? First, we must make a decision to forgive, for God cannot forgive us if we do not forgive others. Jesus says:

> *"Don't pick on people, jump on their failures,*
> *and criticize their faults --- unless, of course,*
> *you want the same treatment. Don't condemn those*
> *who are down; that hardness can boomerang.*
> *Be easy on people; you'll find life a lot easier."*
> *(Luke 6:37 MSG)*

He elaborates in Matthew's Gospel:

> *"For if you forgive men when they sin against you, your*
> *heavenly Father will also forgive you. If you refuse to do*
> *your part, you cut yourself off from God's part."*
> *(Matthew 6:14–15 MSG)*

Secondly, we cannot forgive without the power of the Holy Spirit. It's too hard to do on your own. The Holy Spirit helps us understand, appreciate, and live out God's unconditional forgiveness, teaches us to be merciful as our heavenly Father is merciful, and helps us heal from past rejections, accusations, and abuses.

Thirdly, we need to reflect on the scripture passages that tell us to forgive. A powerful passage is the one where Jesus is dying on the cross. He says, "Father forgive them for they know not what they are doing." Jesus is completely unselfish and asks His Father to forgive Pontius Pilate, the Roman soldiers, the Pharisee, the angry mob, and all of us. Jesus is the sacrificial lamb, who willingly shed His own blood so that we can live. He gave us the benefit of the doubt, by assuming that we have no idea how much harm we do by our actions or inactions. When we have been hurt, betrayed, undermined, or rejected over and over again, we look for revenge. It is at this moment we need to be Christ's students of forgiveness.

Jesus' disciple Peter asks Jesus:

> *"Master, how many times do I forgive*
> *a brother or sister who hurts me? Seven?"*
> *Jesus replied, "Seven! Hardly. Try seventy times seven."*
> *(Matthew 18:21–22 MSG)*

What a challenge, as we think we are saints if we forgive once in a day or even a week or month. Jesus answers in a parable. He tells us a man owed a king ten thousand talents, but he had no money to pay him. The man pleads with the king, and as a result, the King offers forgiveness. This same man then turns on a man who owes him merely a quarter of what he owed the king. When the king hears of it, he is upset and calls the man back. The king takes back his forgiveness, telling the man he should have had mercy on his fellow servant. Then Jesus warns us that this is how our heavenly Father will treat each of us unless we forgive our brother from our heart. Since we have been forgiven so much, we have no right to withhold forgiveness from others. Since we are the debtor forgiven an almost infinite debt, what possible right do we have to not forgive another?

Although there are many other scripture passages to reflect on let's look at a favourite parable:

We can identify well with the prodigal son, for all of us at some time in our life have run away from responsibility, lived a less than a virtuous life, or were concerned only with ourselves. Reflecting on the father of this son, teaches us exactly what it means to forgive. He sees his son coming from afar and runs out to meet him. In other words, he doesn't turn his back and say this son has a nerve to come back after all the hurt he caused. He then hugs his son before the son can fully apologize. Added to this, he tells his servants to get his son a robe, a ring, and sandals. The robe signifies that the father is accepting the son back and has given him the same dignity and honour he had before he went away. He puts a ring on the son's finger. The ring probably has an insignia on it, which will allow the son the same privilege and authority the rest of the family has. Finally, he puts sandals on his feet. Servants in the time of Jesus did not wear shoes, so here, the father is telling the son that he is no longer a slave.

Since the father in this story represents Abba Father, do you see how much He loves us? How He wants us to forgive? He doesn't want us to pay evil back with evil, but with the love that will accept the person back in our lives and treat him/her with respect and dignity.

Pope Francis said that the "joy of God" is ultimately found in pardoning another for his wrongdoing, just as in the parable of the Prodigal

Son. While each of us is the Prodigal Son, who has squandered our own freedom following false idols or mirages of happiness, and has lost everything, God does not forget us. The Father is patient, and He never abandons us. He respects our freedom but always remains faithful. Like the father of the Prodigal Son, when we return to Him, He welcomes us as children, in His house, because He never gives up waiting for us with love, not even for a moment. And His heart is found in the joy that He has for each of us who returns to Him and asks His forgiveness. This same joy would be ours if we could just imitate Jesus' forgiveness and offer our brothers and sisters the same dignity, honour and respect the father gave his son.

We are weak and sinful by nature and as a result at times, unforgiving. This can produce a tendency to judge one another. A prime example of this is what can be referred to as the pack mentality. We find ourselves in a group or gathering of two or more, sharing a common understanding or mutual belief. Then without realizing it, someone in the group will introduce a negative thought about someone outside the group. The common ground that was once positive becomes infected and deteriorates into a wall of accusation that changes the focus of the entire group. We must strive to focus on the details that would lead to a solution to the challenge faced, and not be detoured onto a negative path that becomes destructive.

Our energy sometimes can be misdirected, and we need to catch ourselves with a reversal from negative to positive energy, a reversal of energy from vengefulness or jealousy to one of compassion and helpfulness and unity. Do not ever for a moment discount mercy in the management of your attitude and thinking. At moments such as these, consider the following concise prayer, "Holy Spirit, enable me to see God's image in all men and to serve God in them."

> "Nothing that we despise in other men is inherently
> absent from ourselves.
> We must learn to regard people less in the light of

what they do or don't do,
and more in light of what they suffer."

— Dietrich Bonhoeffer

We are not only called upon to forgive, but we must also be merciful. Mercy is to be kind and forgiving. It is the willingness to help anyone in need, especially in need of pardon or reconciliation. Mercy is poured out on us through the sacrifice of Jesus Christ on the cross.

But mercy is not just what we receive; it is also what we must give.

> *"... we must act justly, love mercy*
> *and walk humbly with our God."*
> *(Micah 6:8 MSG)*

Sadly, we often love mercy only when we *receive* it, but would rather dispense judgement than mercy on others.

As we think about mercy, let us recall that mercy is the ready willingness to help anyone in a time of need, especially through pardon or reconciliation. This means mercy is an attitude on our part, a way of treating others and the world around us, which comes to us automatically in situations. It is giving others compassionate care by taking on the burden of another as our own.

In our everyday lives, opportunities to reach out with compassion occur on a regular basis. We just have to have an open mind and spirit to recognize these moments in time as we are confronted with them.

A case in point would be the events that unfolded in my wife Margaret's life. As a personal support worker, she attended people's homes and assisted them with a myriad of needs including light housework, meals, medication requirements, errands, etc.

At one such private retirement home (nine residents), it became clear that there was a need for someone to take over the administration and day-to-day handling of this home and its residents, as the owner/operators were over- burdened and willing to sell the property. Margaret came home and shared with me the circumstances of these nine people. There was a possibility that their home had the distinct possibility of being downsized and used in a different manner. The people in this home were there because of limited income and the options for this type of resource were few.

As happenstance, would have it, Margaret had been bequeathed a small amount of money. In the spirit of, pay it forward, I suggested that we should use this investment for the continuance of a standard of life to which these nine people had been accustomed. With limited funds and a spirit of wanting to, give something back, we took on the responsibility of this retirement home and its residents. In the nature of giving and the compassion for our fellow brothers and sisters, we have been given an opportunity that is beyond what can be described as self- satisfying. Surely, this little story is an example of the kind of work, the kind of mercy, that God intends each of us to consider as we wind our way through this web of circumstances called life.

The best witness of mercy is Jesus. He revealed God's love to all levels of society by confronting the crowd about to stone the woman taken in adultery, meeting the Samaritan woman at the well, weeping with the other mourners at the death of Lazarus, and ultimately taking up the cross laden with the sins of the world and being led to his death.

> *"… mercy will be the quality*
> *on which the Christian will*
> *ultimately be judged."*
> *(Matthew 25:31–46 MSG)*

Then the King will say to those on His right. Enter, you who are blessed by my Father! Take what's coming to you in this kingdom. It's ready for you since the world's foundation. And here's why:

> *"I was hungry and you fed me,*
> *I was thirsty and you gave me drink,*
> *I was homeless and you gave me a room,*
> *I was shivering and you gave me clothes,*

I was sick and you stopped to visit,
I was in prison and you came to me."
(Matthew 25:34–40 MSG)

Mercy is simply our love's response to suffering. So, the Father of Mercy, to relieve our suffering, sent his Eternal Son to be made flesh by the power of the Holy Spirit. God the Son, by nature incapable of suffering, became vulnerable for us and paid the debt that the human race hadn't been able to cover. His rescue mission succeeded at the cost of his life.

Each day, there are many stories about merciful people in our news broadcast. For example, a woman lost her husband when he set out to buy the morning paper. Her husband was doing what he always did, but this time would not return home. His wife sensed something was wrong and went to look for him. She was greeted by the sight of an ambulance and blood on the ground. Her husband had been struck down by a driver, who was extremely distressed over having hit her husband. She, though, felt no anger towards the driver. She knew that the horrible accident had not been intentional, and she harboured no ill will towards the driver. The sincerity of her forgiveness shone through in a letter she wrote to the driver that was to be used in defending him. In that letter, she wrote, "However bad it was for me, I realize it was 1,000 times worse for you."

The call of Jesus pushes each of us never to stop at the surface of things, especially when we are dealing with a person. We are called to look beyond, to focus on the heart to see how much generosity is possible in everyone. No one can be excluded from the mercy of God.

We are merciful when we live out the corporal and spiritual works of mercy. Let's look at some practical ways to practice these works. We are called today, in the midst of our modern world and busy lives, to look beyond our own busy life and pay attention to those around us who are in need. We can do this by living out the corporal works of mercy, which are to feed the hungry, give drink to the thirsty, clothe the naked, shelter the homeless, visit the sick, ransom the captive, and bury the dead.

These works of mercy are the more practical and visible ways to exercise our faith to those in need. The first and second of these works are closely related. We need to ask ourselves, how often we help provide for the needs of those who are hungry and thirsty? Do we help out at food pantries? Do we donate food or money to buy food for the hungry? Our witness can be extremely powerful by giving "our daily bread" to those who so desperately need it.

We are called to give clothing to the naked. This thought should compel us to consider the excess of clothing that many of us have. How many pairs of shoes do we need? How many pairs of pants and shirts are really necessary for us? Is it possible for us to donate these excesses of ours in order to bring hope to those who need it?

The issue of homelessness is very prominent in our world. A forest fire in Fort McMurray, Alberta, Canada, showed us how devastating homelessness can be. A massive blaze destroyed at least 1,600 homes, businesses, and public buildings. More than 88,000 people had to leave Fort McMurray. Many did not have a home waiting for them when they returned. In total compassion, many throughout the world came to the aid of these grief-stricken people.

Imagine the pain of those who truly have nowhere to go. Are our doors open to those who are in need? Do we offer to take in the homeless? Do we give money to the many shelters that provide such crucial aid to those who are unable to provide for themselves?

We must visit the sick. In doing so, we uphold the dignity of the human person. Consider the feelings of those who spend so much time in hospitals and nursing homes without the comfort of those they love. How many of our elderly are permanently confined to stark buildings, with little love or attention paid to them? We should freely choose to visit the shut-ins, the sick, and the lonely. We can be a great source of hope in their lives.

Another work of mercy is to ransom the captive. How many captives do we know? Today, countless people who are not in jail or being held as a hostage are physically imprisoned in some way or being held hostage by poverty and injustice. Do we help them or pray for them? Consider also the possibilities of visiting the imprisoned. Do we care for those in jail? I once visited a jail, and to my surprise, the prisoners were all young children. They were overjoyed because we brought them chocolate bars. Their pure innocence astounded me. Do we ask how this could happen and what needs to happen before young people get to this stage?

Finally, the last of the corporal works of mercy urges us to bury the dead. It is an act of love to show respect for the bodies of the dead since they were temples of the Holy Spirit during life.

Works of mercy actually help us as well. In so acting, we become changed. Acts of charity destroy selfishness, and happiness grows in our heart. My mother used to say, "When you feel sad, do something nice for someone else," but she was only following Jesus' words, "Give away your life; you'll find life given back, but not merely given back—given back with bonus and blessing. Giving, not getting, is the way. Generosity begets generosity." Luke 6:38 MSG

The Spiritual Works of Mercy are charitable actions by which we come to the aid of our neighbour in spiritual necessities. The seven Spiritual Works of Mercy are: admonish the sinner, instruct the ignorant, counsel the doubtful, comfort the sorrowful, bear wrongs patiently, forgive all injuries, and pray for the living and the dead.

Admonishing the sinner asks us to be courageous yet compassionate in calling people and institutions to be faithful to Gospel values, to intervene in situations in which people are clearly doing harm to themselves or others, and to respond to negative and prejudicial comments with positive statements. Put an end to gossip by asking the originator to pray for the person they are gossiping about.

We are called to instruct the ignorant and counsel the doubtful. We must, therefore, be informed about our faith so that we may properly teach it to those who do not yet know the fullness of the truth.

Comfort the sorrowful means to walk with others through their pain, and to offer words of encouragement and comfort to those who seem discouraged. There are times when all we can do is to give a thoughtful word to someone in pain or sorrow. In doing so, we help others cope with difficulties. We build up the dignity of our brothers and sisters in Christ. Sometimes, people suffer the most when they find no one who is willing to help them in their struggles. They find their dignity and self-worth crushed. Let us never leave a friend in misery without some heartfelt words or a loving embrace to lift them out of their affliction.

We must bear wrongs patiently. This is also a very difficult task because our pride gets in the way. We must not be taken advantage of, says our ego. We must work at being less critical of others, overlook minor flaws and mistakes, and; give people the benefit of the doubt by accepting that people who may have hurt us did so because they are enduring pain of their own. Truly, when others offend us, injure us, attack us, or undermine us, we are called to "turn the other cheek." We can do no better than to imitate Christ, the silent victim, who by His patient, courageous endurance of all forms of bodily and mental torture forgave others. He was beaten, insulted, and killed, yet in His acceptance, He purchased our redemption. How marvellous would our reward be if we could just bear the slightest wrongs with joy and hope in our eternal reward?

Forgiving all injuries means we are to pray for those who have wronged us and pray for the courage to forgive them. When our heart is filled with bitterness and grudges, we find no room for the love of Christ within it. Forgiveness requires heroic virtue at times. Mercy dictates that we forgive others' faults and wrongs, even when it pains us greatly and gives us no satisfaction. Forgiveness is an eternal virtue, as we will find forgiveness after death to the degree that we showed it to others in this life.

Pray for the living and the dead. Pray for the needs of others. Pray for those who have died to be in Heaven. Pray for those who have no one to pray for them.

These works are not optional. They are indeed binding and necessary for our eternal salvation. We are called to be merciful. The opportunities are frequent and urgent. Let us not pass by the afflicted in their times of trial. Let us love others through these spiritual works so that through our sacrifice, we may bring others to the greatest joy, which is the vision of God in His entire splendour in Heaven.

Greater love has no man than this:
that a man lay down his life for his friends.
John 15:13 MSG

CHAPTER 9

LOSING OUR WAY

Our lives here on earth unfold as a result of the designs that we follow in our ultimate goal: the pursuit of happiness. As children, we are blissfully innocent, free of any prejudice, open-minded and free-thinking. There is an aura about us of humility, an inquiring mind (a thirst for knowledge), and a keen attitude for adventure.

As we evolve, grow, and mature to adulthood, the path of life we walk on becomes scattered with the choices we have to make in order to avoid the road blocks that seem to be inevitable as part of our existence. In our everyday life, we are confronted with conflicts that can arise in relationships, an ever-increasing materialistic world, a failure to communicate properly, a failure to develop family values, a world culture of sexual innuendo and pornography that surrounds us, and we are caught up in a treadmill society that seems to be enveloping us.

At first blush, all of this would seem to border on the sensational side of negativity; however, if you think about it long enough and hard enough, you are bound to draw the conclusion that the world we live in is in much need of repair. If you were to paint a picture of the society around you, it would surely resemble a tangled web.

In our pursuit of happiness, we must meet the challenge. *There is a Way!* The combination of the spirit within us and the capacity of the mind can provide amazing results. It is with this God-given gift that we have the ability to meet the challenge through our imagination and reason. Using our memory, we can make a choice—a choice to go to the light. We have the ability to solve complex problems, to imagine new possibilities, and to inhale and enjoy a moment in time such as the beauty of a sunrise. All of this we have the capacity to do! What an awesome gift! Yes, we have challenges, but we also have gifts. However, because of our sinful nature, we do have a dark side as well, and sometimes that dark side causes us to say and do harmful things. We sometimes allow our minds to take us to the darkness that is much like a cat, waiting to pounce and overcome the moment.

What we have to realize is that the spirit within us is ready and willing to go to the light, but all too often the flesh is weak, and the inevitable outcome is that we succumb to the properties of our self-centredness and sinful nature. Simply put, if we allow the darkness to prevail, it most certainly will. It is essential that we follow our inner spirit and listen! Listen! Listen! The path of that light will most assuredly lead us in the direction of our Maker, the One who created us, our God!

Our Guide and Protector are found through a relationship that is based on the perseverance of faith and prayer. Submit yourselves, then, to God. Resist the devil, and he will flee from you. Come near to God, and He will come near to you. Wash your hands, you sinners, and purify your hearts, you double-minded.

If Satan (the power of darkness) has his way, we will become side-tracked with external influences and distractions, which are fast becoming a way of life in this wayward society that is slowly moving towards a Godless society. History is marching towards a repeat chapter in the life and times of the fall of the Roman empire. In all that we do and all that we are, we become subject to and slaves of the choices we make. What is required through the perseverance of faith and prayer is a revival of the soul!

Recently, I attended a retreat led by our Bishop, Michael Mulhall. He referred to renewal as a tool to be used in the revival of our soul. The story he told us was as a young boy he went with his father out into the bush to cut wood. He stood in awe, as his dad, on each occasion, would take the axe down from the truck and tediously scrape and clean any rust or tarnish from the axe. This always took a goodly amount of time. When he questioned his father about this procedure, he was told to always have his working tools clean, ready, and in good order to complete the job at hand.

The Bishop used this analogy in describing the challenge each of us has in reviving our soul to a state of renewal, the renewal of our spiritual selves, the renewal of our souls! There is a tarnish attached to our souls, but as long as we continue to polish our souls, in an attempt to reach purity, we are doing our job. We are, each of us, a work in progress! We have to shed our outer skins, those skins causing us darkness that can come over us and take hold of our very being.

How do we revive the soul? By *allowing* the shafts of light, *the light of God*, to stream right through! The light in the lamp of our souls must be made to shine—to shine—to shine!

The world may at times seem to be a tangled web, but behind it all is the love of God, a love that has absolutely no limitations.

> *"Only where God is seen does life truly begin.*
> *Only when we meet the living God in Christ,*
> *do we know what life is. We are not some casual*
> *and meaningless product of evolution.*
> *Each of us is the result of a thought of God.*
> *Each of us is willed. Each of us is loved.*
> *Each of us is necessary. There is nothing*
> *more beautiful than to be surprised by the Gospel,*
> *by the encounter with Christ.*
> *There is nothing more beautiful than to know Him*
> *and to speak to others of our friendship with Him."*

— Pope Benedict XVI

Our faith and our prayer make us aware that this phase of our life here on earth is fleeting and one that passes quickly. One might refer to our present life as a stepping stone or a continuation of a life that is beyond our ability to comprehend.

It is our responsibility to address the whole aspect of an eternal perspective, which definitely exists and which, for the most part, we have not explored to the extent that we should. We must prepare ourselves for the next leg of the journey.

A rose withers and dies, but its roots lie in wait for a second coming. Our lives here on earth are similar, and in the same way, the gardener fertilizes the soil, we must prepare our spirits for advancement. The hardship and suffering that we are presently experiencing is nothing more than a time of preparation for what is to come.

The challenges in this life are many. We all have them. We must turn to our God-given gifts, concentrating on the positives in our lives and using the gifts we have at our disposal, turning towards the light and not dwelling or allowing the darkness to envelop us.

We live in a materialistic world that has almost entirely lost its eternal perspective. We need to take a long-term view and understand that the suffering we endure in this world must be viewed and understood in the context of eternity. *That eternity is now!* Losing our way is not an option! It's time to prepare, to make ready, and to scrape away the tarnish, to polish and revive the soul!

> *"Don't look for shortcuts to God. The market is flooded with surefire, easygoing formulas for a successful life that can be practiced in your spare time. Don't fall for that stuff, even though crowds of people do. The way to life—to God! — is vigorous and requires total attention."*
> (Matthew 7:13–14 MSG)

Heaven is a place where we will go after our work for Christ on this earth is through. Heaven will be our reward when we've done what He has called us to do, and have shared God's love with others. Although this is true, it seems to have little bearing on the average Christian life. We are comfortable to call ourselves Christians if we go to church on Sunday but leave God out for the rest of the week. We like the idea of going to Heaven, but we are procrastinators. We convince ourselves that we have lots of time so we will get ready for Heaven later when we are older, but not yet.

> *"You call out to God for help and He helps —He's a good Father that way. But don't forget, He's also a responsible Father, and won't let you get by with sloppy living."*
> (1 Peter 1:17 MSG)

We need to be careful how we live out our lives. We need to show in our words and actions that we know God and love Him. You may be the only Bible many people will ever read. You are to be a light to the world!

"You're not getting by with anything. Every refusal and avoidance of God adds fuel to the fire. The day is coming when it's going to blaze hot and high, God's fiery and righteous judgment. Make no mistake: In the end you get what's coming to you—Real Life for those who work on God's side, but to those who insist on getting their own way and take the path of least resistance, Fire!

If you go against the grain, you get splinters, regardless of which neighborhood you're from, what your parents taught you, what schools you attended. But if you embrace the way God does things, there are wonderful payoffs, again without regard to where you are from or how you were brought up. Being a Jew won't give you an automatic stamp of approval. God pays no attention to what others say (or what you think) about you.
He makes up his own mind."
(Romans 2:6–11 MSG)

Jesus said,

"I am the Road, also the Truth, also the Life.
No one gets to the Father apart from me."
(John 14:6 MSG)

He also said,

"I came so they can have real and eternal life,
more and better life than they ever dreamed of."
(John 10:10 MSG)

The surprising factor is not everyone wants what is required to live this abundant life. The real disciples of Jesus must have a heart big enough to love God and totally depend on Him. We need to surrender ourselves to the Holy Spirit so we may obey what He says. Sounds easy, but we don't like anyone to tell us what to do, even if it's God! Surrendering ourselves to the Holy Spirit means to allow the Spirit of God and the Word of God to tell us what to do.

Matthew's message is not a very consoling message for Christians who think they can just coast into Heaven by fulfilling their Sunday obligation or by calling themselves Christians. Jesus showed us, when He lived on earth, how to fit through a narrow gate. He didn't only talk about the Kingdom of God, but also lived it. He gave of Himself, day after day, by healing the sick, comforting the grieving, and showing God's merciful love to all He met.

To be able to enter a narrow door, we have to drop our baggage, or we won't fit through the door. Money will not get us through the door, nor will fame, nor popularity. The actor Jim Carrey once said, "I wish everyone could become rich and famous so they will know that this is not the answer." We need to drop our pride, our resentments, our know-it-all attitude, and our jealousies, and become doers of God's Word. To gain admittance means we will shed our indifferences, our prejudices, our hatreds, and our personal agendas.

> "A devout life does bring wealth, but it's the rich simplicity
> of being you before God. Since we entered the world
> penniless and will leave it penniless, if we have bread on
> the table and shoes on our feet, that's enough. But if it's
> only money these leaders are after, they'll self-destruct in
> no time. Lust for money brings trouble and nothing but
> trouble. Going down that path, some lose their footing in
> the faith completely and live to regret it bitterly ever after."
> (1 Timothy: 6–10 MSG)

A book that came out in 1950, *The Man Who Got Even with God*, gives us a memorable example of how we can turn from the wide door to the narrow door. It is a story of John Hanning, a hotheaded person who out of anger took revenge on his violent father. He burned down the barn, which housed the tobacco that provided a living for his family. In John's mind, he was getting even with his father.

John then becomes a cowboy and was not friends with anyone. After many years of roaming he, like the Prodigal Son, comes home and reconciles with his family. Realizing how unloving he has become in his ways, he decides to get even with God by entering the Trappist monastery. Here he was known as Brother Joachim, and his life totally transformed. If you read his story not only will you find yourself in his words and actions, but you will also find yourself accepting John as your hero.

Most of us want to choose the narrow door, but when we think about living out the Ten Commandments, the Beatitudes, and a responsible Christian life, we start asking: "Did God really ask us to forgive our enemies? Or to tell the truth? Or forgive seventy times seven in one day?" Sin always looks good, like the icing on a cake, and we end up choosing the wide door.

When Adam and Eve committed the first sin, they passed the potential for sin on to all future descendants for all generations. Adam and Eve wanted to determine for themselves what constituted good and what constituted evil. They chose to reject God and His abundant love.

The Greeks use the word *hamartia* to describe sin. It means to miss the mark. To understand this description, imagine that in the centre of the target are the words "love God with all your heart" and "love your neighbour as yourself." Each morning, as we get up, we are ready to aim and hit this target. Sounds easy, but the rough and tough world we live in makes it difficult to always hit the centre of the target. For instance, you come to the breakfast table, and your wife tells you that when she backed into the garage last night, she hit the door and knocked it off. As you respond to her, how close do you get to the centre of the target?

Every day, we have a choice. Will we open our hearts and allow the Holy Spirit to reign over them, or will we continue to strive to get only what we want and remain in our sin?

However,

> *"If we claim that we're free of sin, we're only fooling ourselves. A claim like that is errant nonsense. On the other hand, if we admit our sins—make a clean breast of them—He won't let us down; He'll be true to Himself. He'll forgive our sins and purge us of all wrongdoing. If we claim that we've never sinned, we out-and-out contradict God—make a liar out of Him. A claim like that only shows off our ignorance of God."*
> *(1 John 1:9–10) MSG*

There is no sin too great that cannot be forgiven. The Bible tells us how God forgave Paul after he murdered Christians, forgave the woman caught in adultery, and welcomed back the prodigal son.

Luke tells us The Story of the Lost Coin:

> *"… imagine a woman who has ten coins and loses one. Won't she light a lamp and scour the house, looking in every nook and cranny until she finds it? And when she finds it you can be sure she'll call her friends and neighbors: 'Celebrate with me! I found my lost coin!' Count on it—that's the kind of party God's angels throw every time one lost soul turns to God."*
> *(Luke 15: 8–10 MSG)*

We say the "Our Father" and are reminded to forgive others so we may be forgiven. We saw a powerful example of such forgiveness on the news this year, when the families of the Charleston killer offered forgiveness to the young man who killed their relatives as they attended a Bible study group. These relatives were true witnesses of God's love. They showed they chose the narrow gate, not the gate of revenge and anger. God calls us to imitate Him by being merciful and loving to all those we meet.

CHAPTER 10

SUFFERING

The path that leads us to the Light of Christ is not always easy. We must learn that sometimes we encounter a teacher along the way, a teacher who comes to us in the form of suffering.

A man in his seventies paces the floor night after night, tormented with a lack of forgiveness by a family member. It has been months since he has been able to sleep properly!

A young lady in her mid-twenties laments and agonizes over a personal predicament. She doesn't know who to turn to. She is heard to say, "I had no idea that life would turn out like this!"

A woman who is comfortable and secure in the material things of this world leaves a doctor's office feeling isolated and alone as she has been diagnosed with life-threatening cancer!

These are just three stories of suffering and sickness that could very well happen to anyone of us: a member of our family, a close friend, or a neighbour. Every one of us will suffer at one time or another, throughout our lives. We are all in need of healing, whether it is spiritual or physical healing.

Suffering in itself is neither good nor bad. We do not like suffering ourselves, nor do we like to see others suffer. Suffering entered our world due to sin. God did not create it. So, you ask, why then does God allow suffering?

- Suffering is our invitation to share in His Passion.

- The book of Proverbs tells us that God allows us to suffer in order to help us become holy.

- As well, Hebrews tells us:

> *"God is educating you; that's why you must never drop out. He's treating you as dear children. This trouble is not punishment; it's training, the normal experience of children .... While we were children, our parents did what seemed best to them. But God is doing what is best for us, training us to live God's holy best."*
> *(Hebrews 12:5-11 MSG)*

Suffering has a value. Sometimes God allows us to undergo sickness as a form of discipline and training in virtue and justice. St. Paul himself learned this when he prayed three times that God would remove a handicap from him. God answered, "My grace is enough; it's all you need." (2 Corinthians 1:2:9 MSG)

At first, Paul didn't think this was much of a gift, but he soon realized that it was in his weakness that Christ made him stronger.

If Paul had not become ill while on his first missionary journey and been forced to stop travelling, he would not have preached to the Galatians, for he tells them, "...the reason I ended up preaching to you was that I was physically broken, and so, prevented from continuing my journey, I was forced to stop with you." (Galatians 4:13. MSG)

If he had not preached to the Galatians, he would not have later written them the letter that appears in our New Testament. God used Paul's illness to bring salvation to the Galatians and to bring us a work of scripture from which we are still benefitting today. Here we can see that suffering can bring about a good. If we offer our sufferings in union with

Jesus' suffering, we not only bring out the good in ourselves but will receive great graces and blessings from God.

In our suffering, the Wisdom of God prevails! In the midst of our doubts, fears, and anxieties, and, yes, even pain, the following thought prevails: the love with which Christ suffered to redeem us is continually witnessed in our own suffering as we share not only the love of Christ, but also in the passion of Christ. Paul says in his letter to the Colossians:

> "I welcome the chance to take my share in the church's part of that suffering. When I became a servant in this church, I experienced this suffering as a sheer gift, God's way of helping me serve you, laying out the whole truth". (Colossians 1: 24 MSG)

Is it not only natural that if we enter into a love affair with Jesus Christ, that we also share in his suffering? Suffering (if we allow it to) can be the seeking out and then taking on of the light of Christ. Handing ourselves over to Christ, we transform our thinking into a clear understanding and comprehension of what suffering can produce. We allow the Spirit of Christ to become part of our suffering. This process then cleanses and opens our mind to the positive aspects of suffering. We learn patience, love, understanding, perseverance, acceptance, wisdom, peace, sharing, strength, and humility.

Joni Eareckson Tada shows us how suffering has brought her closer to Christ. She says:

> "My weakness, that is, my quadriplegia, is my greatest asset because it forces me into the arms of Christ every single morning when I get up"

Joni Eareckson and her sister went for a swim. The result was tragic. Joni dove into shallow water, struck her head on a rock, and became a quadriplegic, paralyzed from the neck down.

At times, Joni was angry with God, but she learned that it is in her weakness that God's strength can shine through.

One night, God came close to Joni, and she understood that God loved her. She realized that Jesus understood her as He had gone through the suffering of being paralyzed on the cross.

Today, Joni is married, a painter (she paints with her mouth), a singer, and a songwriter. She spends her time helping others who are paralyzed know that life is still worth living.

Paintings by Joni Eareckson Tada

The healing ministry of Jesus is directly connected with suffering. In Mark's Gospel, we find Jesus carrying out activities that draw a very clear picture for us. Christ moves increasingly closer to the world of human suffering! He went about His ministry and His actions brought about the healing of those who were suffering.

He healed the sick, consoled the afflicted, fed the hungry, freed people from deafness, from blindness, from leprosy, from the devil, and from various physical disabilities. Three times He restored the dead to life. He was sensitive to every human suffering, whether of the body or of the soul.

We all have a bridge of faith to cross! A journey that includes pain and suffering that is to be shared with Jesus Christ! It is for us as followers of Christ to share in the sufferings of Christ!

The following words are from John Paul II's 1984 *Apostolic Letter, SALVIFICI DOLORIS*:

> *"In the eyes of the just God, before his judgment, those*
> *who share in the suffering of Christ become worthy of this*
> *Kingdom. Through their sufferings, in a certain sense they*
> *repay the infinite price of the Passion and death of Christ,*
> *which became the price of our Redemption... "*

In this hurry-up world we live in, it is the vulnerability through sickness and suffering that leads us directly to a meaningful "one on one" relationship with Jesus.

When Jewish psychiatrist Victor Frankl was arrested by the Nazis in World War II, he was stripped of everything: property, family, and possessions. A few days later, when the Nazis forced the prisoners to give up their clothes, he lost the manuscript to a book he was writing. He was given the worn-out rags of an inmate who had been sent to the gas chamber. He found in the pocket of the newly acquired rags a single page torn out of a Hebrew prayer book, which contained the main Jewish prayer, "Shema Yisrael" (Hear, O Israel! The Lord our God is one God. And you shall love the Lord your God with all your heart and with all your soul.) He decided then to take up this challenge and to live out this prayer. Later, as Frankl reflected on his ordeal, he wrote in his book, *Man's Search for Meaning*:

> *"There is nothing in the world, I venture to say, that would*
> *so effectively help one to survive, even the worst conditions,*
> *as the knowledge that there is a meaning in one's life. There*
> *is much wisdom in the words of Nietzsche: ""He who has a*
> *why, to live for can bear almost any how."*

Recently, I found myself bed-ridden with pneumonia and I was at a low ebb, which allowed me to share with God my sickness and struggle for renewal. During this process, I found myself closer to my Lord and Saviour than at any other time in my life. For when we are powerless, it is then that we are strong.

I found myself dealing with my past life and facing up to a forgiveness of self and asking God for forgiveness. To ask for forgiveness or to forgive someone is like taking medicine for an illness and getting immediate, positive results. Through our thoughts, words, or actions we may hurt someone or they in turn may have done us harm. To share forgiveness is very much a healing process and is food for the soul.

To say "I am sorry"—two simple words—can move mountains of mis-understanding and provide healing.

And so, it is in our relationship with God! Forgiveness and healing should be the fabric of our daily lives. We need to look no further than to witness the work of Jesus, which is also our work!

All of this steeped in faith, the faith of God's healing love for each of us, allowing us to share our suffering with the suffering of Christ.

In some way or another, we are all wounded, and at times we wound those around us. We are all in need of healing: Jesus' work of healing bodies and souls, minds and hearts, and his merciful treatment of sinners. The sick throughout history help each of us understand that our sickness and suffering is definitely a bridge of faith. It is a reminder that we not only share in the Body of Christ, but we share in Jesus' continuing work today. If we are one in Christ, do we share in the sufferings of Christ?

Amid all that ails us, God's loving intention is for our well-being. However, we are not left alone in our suffering, for we have the Holy Spirit to be with us to strengthen and encourage us.

Jesus' healing miracles and exorcisms raise the hope of Resurrection in all of us amid life's worst challenges!

Often times, have you heard the question, "Why is there suffering in the world?" If you stop and consider all that God has created and consider the Wisdom of God in relation to suffering, the next words shine light on the answer:

"Without suffering, there would be no compassion."

— Nicholas Sparks

Please allow me to share with you an act of faith entitled "The Price of Admission."

"When the strong fall, what hope is there for the weak?
Thus reasons the unthinking man.
"Oh," God sighed, not knowing what else to do.
"Have I been with you so long and you do not understand?
It is in your weakness that my strength is revealed,
It is when you are sick that you come to me to be healed.
It was from the fabric of nothingness, I created each star.
It was from nothingness, I formed the masterpiece you are.
If weakness teaches you this - that to me you belong.
Then your weakness has not made you weak,
It has made you strong.
So come to me and I will give you strength.
More than this, I will give you life without length.
I will give you the keys opening beyond the doors of strife, I
will welcome you into the banquet of everlasting life."

— Anonymous

Through all of this—a share in the cross of Christ!

Sometimes, our thought processes cause a suffering of the mind that holds us captive. My aunt Helena (my Mother's sister), one of nine children brought up by my grandparents, was intimidated by the rigid rules of family life set forth especially by my grandfather. In her youth, Helena met a young man, and they fell in love. She did not know how to break the news to her father that she and her friend were planning marriage.

They were convinced of his strenuous objection to this union. So, taking matters into their own hands, they secretly went out and were married.

During this time and for quite a period of time following this marriage, Helena continued to hold this secret within her mind and within her heart. She stayed living in the family home, subject to her mother and father. Unfortunately, she allowed this little secret to envelop her, and this gave way to depression and a relentless melancholy that eventually compounded itself into a prison of suffering. She shared these events of her life with no other living soul. This very lack of communication ended up with her being committed to an institution.

There are many forms of suffering, but the point of this story is to remind all of us to know in our heart of hearts that we are not alone! We must condition, open and cleanse our minds to the fact that we can and should turn all the events of our lives over to Jesus Christ, our Redeemer and Saviour. He is not only our Redeemer and Saviour, but He is our friend, a friend who expects and welcomes this type of communication, a relationship that is ever loving and everlasting.

"Seek and you shall find!" (Matthew 11:7 MSG)

CHAPTER 11

FLESH AND SPIRIT

**Within each of us is the challenge of what
God has created and what man has created.**

There is an instinct in all of us to survive!

What exactly is it that we are trying to maintain?

The body that houses us has been aptly described as a temple. It is a resting place for our souls.

The world that we inhabit encourages us and almost dictates that during the central or mid-life part of our existence, there is a period that is concentrated on the values of society, greed, individualism, the idols of power, money, competition, and our outward appearance ("the body beautiful").

Any success or notoriety that one is expected to achieve is based on materialistic wealth, power, or gain. Our educational system has all but blocked any and all spiritual or inner depth approach to mind development. Towards the end of our earthly lives, we are encouraged to prepare for our demise in planning cremation as a final resting place for the body, the temple.

Taking these facts into consideration, should we not then be turning our focus to a higher level of our existence on the maintenance of the central part of our being our very spirit, the survival of the soul?

Within our lifetime, we will experience personal body breakdown in the form of disease, cancer, organ malfunctions, etc. *This body of ours–this temple–is temporary!*

God created us to go far beyond the "speck of time" that is our earthly existence. God created us as precious and everlasting in building each of us as an edifice of spirit.

There is one inescapable fact in the form that God has created, *what is born of the flesh is flesh, and what is born of the spirit is spirit!*

Saint Paul, in his letter to the Ephesians, refers to a plan, of the mystery hidden for ages in God who created all things,

> *"All this is proceeding along lines planned all along by*
> *God and then executed in Christ Jesus. When we trust in*
> *him, we're free to say whatever needs to be said, bold to go*
> *wherever we need to go. So, don't let my present trouble on*
> *your behalf get you down. Be proud!*

My response is to get down on my knees before the Father,
this magnificent Father who parcels out all heaven and
earth. I ask him to strengthen you by his Spirit—not a
brute strength but a glorious inner strength—that Christ
will live in you as you open the door and invite him in.
And I ask him that with both feet planted firmly on love,
you'll be able to take in with all followers of Jesus the
extravagant dimensions of Christ's love.
Reach out and experience the breadth! Test its length!
Plumb the depths! Rise to the heights!
Live full lives, full in the fullness of God."
(Ephesians 3: 12-21 MSG)

The phrase St. Paul uses "to comprehend the breadth and length and height and depth" expresses the enormity of the mystery.

Saint Augustine interprets these words "as referring to the Cross, the instrument of salvation which Christ used to show the full extent of his love." (The theology of signs in St. Augustine's *De doctrina christiana*, 2, 41.)

Saint Paul may indeed be trying to sum up all the richness of the mystery of Christ in a graphic way in terms of a Cross whose extremities reach out in all four directions, seeking to embrace the whole world. (*Navarre Bible*, "Captivity Letters").

The words, "That you may be strengthened in your inner self with power through His Spirit," speak to the fusing of *our* spirit to the Spirit of God.

And the phrase "… and that Christ may dwell in your hearts through faith, as you are being rooted and grounded in love …" speaks to the seed of that Spirit that has been planted in each of us.

All of this supports the often-used phrase through prayer, "We are one in Christ."

The challenge for all of us is to 'weed out', the fleshly, materialistic part of our beings and concentrate on the much more rewarding nourishment of our soul.

Only by speaking deeply to our consciences (the spirit within us) can that spirit move us to separate darkness from light. Only by living by the Word of Jesus and imprinting that way, that truth, and that life on our hearts can we be filled with the spirit of consolation, peace, and joy. Only by filling ourselves with the love of God can the Spirit soften our hearts and move us to love one another with the breadth, and length, and height, and depth that is expressed in the love of the Cross.

So, what, therefore, is our job while on earth? St. Paul, in his letter to the Corinthians, reminds us,

> *"You realize, don't you, that you are the temple of God,*
> *and God himself is present within you? ... you can*
> *be sure of that. God's temple is sacred—and you,*
> *remember, are the temple."*
> *(1 Corinthians 3:17 MSG)*

Peter, the apostle, goes on to say, God said, "I am holy; you be holy. (1Peter 1:16 MSG)

What, then, does it mean to be holy? To be holy simply means to be set apart for a special purpose by God. Just as God made the Israelites His Chosen People (separated from those around them), God made us His special children, His own, through baptism. Our job on earth, therefore, is to strive for opportunities to become more like Him, to strive for opportunities to grow in holiness or more simply, to become a saint. When we don't follow God's path to holiness, we will find life pointless and empty.

Some believe that to be holy means to withdraw from the world or to spend our days on our knees praying or to never smile or enjoy the now. The opposite, however, is true.

Living a holy life means to become all God wants us to be. It means to allow our decisions to be guided by the Holy Spirit and to surrender to what God wants. Holiness doesn't happen by accident. It is a gift from God, and it doesn't happen overnight. Following the life of St. Paul, we see he didn't go from being a persecutor to a saint overnight. He had to face his own temptations and sins. He says:

> *"What I want to do, I do not do, but what I hate I do."*
> *(Romans 7:15 MSG)*

Pope Francis tells us "holiness doesn't mean doing extraordinary things, but doing ordinary things with faith and love."

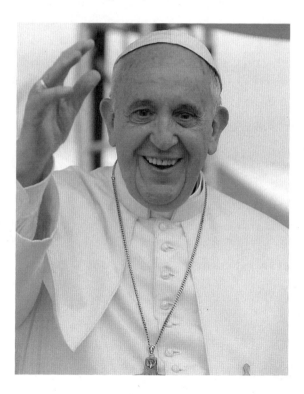

Holiness, therefore, requires us to serve the poor, pray without ceasing, and share the Good News through our words and actions.

Sometimes we need a push from the Holy Spirit to spur us on our journey towards holiness. As we work towards sainthood, we will not look physically different or sprout angel wings, but we will slowly deepen our relationship with God so that we will be able to die to self and live for God.

Archbishop Oscar Romeo was chosen to be Archbishop of San Salvador because he was a safe bet. He sided with the government, respected the wealthy landowners, supported the church hierarchy, and would therefore not upset the small group that controlled the government.

Archbishop Romeo became the government's worst enemy after his friend, Fr. Rutillo Grande, was murdered by this same government for advocating for the poor. He gave up attending state celebrations and meetings and instead worked tirelessly for the poor and forgotten. He pleaded in his sermons for the soldiers to stop their violence and even wrote to Jimmy Carter, President of the US, and to the UN, and to Rome, asking them to stop helping the army by sending them weapons, but his pleas were never heard.

In 1980, Romero was assassinated while offering Mass. No one has ever been charged with his murder.

Oscar Romero is a hero for us because he gave voice to those without a voice, and stood with and encouraged those who had lost all hope. His whole life was seemingly insignificant until his last few years when he listened to and acted upon his conscience, which changed the future of an entire nation.

St. Catherine of Sienna tells us we too can make changes in our lives, for she says:

> *"You, God, are a fire that takes away the coldness,*
> *illuminates the mind with its light, and causes me to*
> *know your truth and I know that you are beauty and*
> *wisdom itself."*

In our lifetime, there are many stories of people who have changed from living a life for success, money, or power to living lives of doing what God wants them to do. One such person was Mother Teresa, who became St. Teresa of Calcutta.

When Agnes (St. Teresa) was eighteen years old, she felt God wanted her to become a nun. She entered the Sisters of Loreto in Ireland. She was sent to Calcutta to teach in a wealthy girl's school for fifteen years. Although happy teaching, she felt God wanted her to go out on the streets of Calcutta and look after the poor and dying who had no one to care for them. With this desire in her heart, she left the Sisters of Loreto and started the Order of the Missionaries of Charity, a Roman Catholic congregation of women dedicated to helping the poor.

She started out small by opening a school for five poor children and went into the homes of the poor to help them.

Mother Teresa, and those who later joined her, wanted those who were forgotten, left to die alone, or were on the fringes of society to know God loved them through their charity.

St. Teresa died in 1997, but when we think of her, we can learn all we need to know about love. It doesn't take money, or popularity, or intelligence; it only takes love. She tells us,

> *"I am not sure exactly what heaven will be like, but I know that when we die and it comes time for God to judge us, he will not ask, "How many good things have you done in your life?" rather he will ask, "How much love did you put into what you did?"*

— St. Teresa of Calcutta

St. Paul, in the Acts of the Apostles, goes on to say:

> *"I feel compelled to go to Jerusalem ... I'm completely in the dark about what will happen when I get there. I do know that it won't be any picnic, for the Holy Spirit has let me know repeatedly and clearly that there are hard times and imprisonment ahead. But that matters little. What matters most to me is to finish what God started: the job the Master Jesus gave me of letting everyone I meet know all about this incredibly extravagant generosity of God."*
> *(Acts 20:24 MSG)*

To know (knowledge), to understand (gain wisdom), to grow and move towards a relationship that sows the seeds of eternal love and peace— there is a relationship that is there for the taking ... *within us!*

CHAPTER 12

INCARNATION

The Incarnation of Jesus, making him both human and divine, can be described as an invitation to each of us from our Creator to follow in the footsteps of Jesus. To be human is to live out our lives caring for our body, those around us, and this earth we dwell on with compassion and tender, loving attention. It is to care for the human form.

As Jesus is divine, through the process of His Incarnation, we have only to imitate the divine life of Jesus, which would have us follow the path that He took.

The invitation from God is for each of us to cultivate not only our humanity, but our divinity as well. To be divine is to relate to God.

Our reason, intellect, and logic guide us in those decisions, and they become human in their outcome … not then decisions based on our divinity (our closeness to God), but decisions that result in an external or human conclusion that leaves God excluded from the equation.

We live out our lives in shades of human strengths and weaknesses. All too often we allow ourselves to be subject to doubts, fears, and anxieties that block our inner divinity and block our path to saving grace, a path that is the way, the truth, and the life … a guide to our salvation.

**Every day of our lives we make choices that determine
the direction of our lives.**

An example of this is found in a conversation I had with "J" (full name omitted), who I visited in the hospice section of a hospital as I did my visitation rounds. This was a man in his early seventies who, knowing he had a limited amount of time left on this earth, described himself as having an undue amount of anguish, causing him to be unsettled and in some discomfort.

As I attempted to console him, I asked him if he was comfortable in sharing with me the source of his anguish. He described to me a life that included a Christian upbringing that changed direction in mid-life, because of what he pointed to as "issues."

"If you don't mind me asking," I inquired, "What were these issues?"

There was a lengthy pause, and then he said, "My sexuality." He went on, saying, "I have always loved the ladies ..."

"J" was a good-looking, articulate individual who went on to describe a search throughout his life for a God that eluded him as he searched for answers to an issue in his life that would offer him self-satisfying solutions. He was not finding those answers within the doctrines and teachings of his Christian faith.

The path that "J" chose to take was to follow a pattern in his life that allowed him to follow his physical needs at the expense of turning his back on his Creator.

"J" passed away before we were able to resume a planned follow-up to that conversation. I can only pray that he was able to reconcile his life here on earth in finally accepting the love and forgiveness of God into his life before he took his last worldly breath.

Some people who turned away from God were also able to change their hearts and begin a deeper relationship with Him. One such person was Alison (not her real name).

Alison left the church because she decided that the Christian life with all its laws was just too hard for her. For the next four years, she used her God-given gifts to live an extravagant and luxurious lifestyle. She drank heavily, verbally abused anyone who got in her way, and filled herself with sex and material things so she could forget her Christian training.

All this did not win her friends or fill her with happiness. In fact, due to unforeseen circumstances, she lost everything.

Then she felt God was calling her back to Him. She realized that when she chose to be reckless and irresponsible with God's gifts, she was acting as a prodigal child. What she hadn't realized before was that God dwelt within her. When she told God she would be in charge of her own life and make her own decisions, she had only seen God as a demanding law keeper, not as an unconditional lover. Although she could tell you the answers to many religious questions, she had never really had a personal relationship with Him.

With the help of a friend, she learned that the Holy Spirit given to her at her baptism would not only guide her to a deeper relationship with God, but would also help her use her gifts to further His Kingdom.

After four years, Alison had a change of heart. She no longer wanted to continue to live as she had. Alison repented. Just as in the Gospel story of the Prodigal Son, Alison was reminded that no matter how far we wander away from God or how many of God's gifts we waste, we can always come home to Him. The Lord is always waiting with open arms.

No one has turned so far away from God that they cannot come home to Him.

Dismas, the good thief, shows us that even at the moment of death, repentance and forgiveness are possible. We do not know what crime he committed, but it must have been bad enough to be punished by crucifixion.

All Dismas said to Jesus was:

> "...remember me when you come into your kingdom."
> Jesus said, "Don't worry, I will. Today you will
> join me in paradise."
> (Luke 23:42–43 MSG)

Dismas is the patron saint of the dying, prisoners, and funeral directors. His feast day is celebrated on March 25th.

> "Knowing the correct password—saying 'Master, Master,'
> for instance—isn't going to get you anywhere with me.
> What is required is serious obedience—doing what my
> Father wills. I can see it now—at the Final Judgment
> thousands strutting up to me and saying, 'Master, we
> preached the Message, we bashed the demons, our God-
> sponsored projects had everyone talking.' And do you know
> what I am going to say? 'You missed the boat. All you did
> was use me to make yourselves important. You don't impress
> me one bit. You're out of here.'

*"These words I speak to you are not incidental additions
to your life, homeowner improvements to your standard
of living. They are foundational words, words to build a
life on. If you work these words into your life, you are like
a smart carpenter who built his house on solid rock. Rain
poured down, the river flooded, a tornado hit—but nothing
moved that house. It was fixed to the rock.*

*"But if you just use my words in Bible studies and
don't work them into your life, you are like a stupid
carpenter who built his house on the sandy beach.
When a storm rolled in and the waves came up,
it collapsed like a house of cards."*
(Matthew 7: 21–27 MSG)

Christianity is a religion of hope, not despair. Our God can come as close to us as we want if we open our heart to Him. He showers us with His love, compassion, and joy. He asks only that we imitate Him and His love in our world today.

Let's look at what the incarnation means for us. First, it tells us of the miracle of God's love for us. He loved us so much He sent His only Son to die for us so we would have eternal life. To have someone die for us demonstrates how important each individual is. We can also see that God is not a distant ruler who is not concerned about us, but rather, in the words of St. Paul, is a ruler who "emptied" Himself in order to become one of us.

Jesus came to earth as a tiny baby born in a poor stable. He was raised in a family where He obeyed His mother and earthly father.

He lived in Nazareth. A run-down, scoffed at place from whence nothing good was expected to emerge. Jesus played and toiled in these surroundings, facing all the stresses and opportunities of a person, much like any one of us. As a result of this upbringing, Jesus can always identify with our plight in life. For us, this is a consolation that Jesus can understand us more than we comprehend.

During Jesus' ministry on earth, we see Him facing conflict, betrayal, temptation, and frustration. In all these instances, He by His example shows us how to live and how to love. Looking through the Gospel stories, we see that Jesus never held a grudge. He was a forgiver. He forgave unconditionally. We see this when He forgave the adulterous woman and healed those everyone else ran away from. He repaired the damage our sin brings to the world.

Wonderful things happen to us as a result of Jesus being human. We share in the holiness of God, and we can have an intimate relationship with Him. Sickness, suffering, mourning, and death will not have the last word, for Jesus made it possible for us to go to Heaven.

The divine life that is within us is a gift from God to be used in the same way that Jesus combined his human and divine life as He walked the face of the earth, taking on human form. Jesus was obedient to his Father in all his thoughts, words, and actions.

The life of Jesus is for us a prototype (the ultimate role model) of a plan that is our road map to an eternal life of salvation.

> *The prescription, then, for a life fully lived,*
> *both human and divine, is summed up in the words,*
> *"That you love the Lord your God with all your passion*
> *and prayer and muscle and intelligence—and that*
> *you love your neighbor as well as you do yourself."*
> *(Luke 10:27 MSG)*

Our pilgrimage on this earth is to include perseverance and be diligent in combining our humanity with an approach to becoming divine.

CHAPTER 13

DISCIPLINE

Our spiritual journey is a process. For a Christian, this journey will be serious, challenging, and demanding. St. Paul, in his letter to Timothy, says:

> *"Exercise daily in God. No spiritual flabbiness, please!*
> *Workouts in the gymnasium are useful, but*
> *a disciplined life in God is far more so,*
> *making you fit both today and forever."*
> *(Timothy 4:7 MSG)*

If we ever hope of having a passion for improving the quality of our life and attaining holiness, we must start on the path of spiritual discipline.

In the New Testament, we find two different meanings for the word *discipline*. The first meaning that comes to mind is punishment for some wrongdoing. Discipline can also mean to train oneself to do the right thing or to form habits that will lead us to holiness.

St. Paul helps us to understand this second definition of discipline when he compares self-discipline to an athlete who is training to compete in the ancient athletic games:

> *"You've all been to the stadium and seen the athletes race.*
> *Everyone runs; one wins. Run to win. All good athletes*

train hard. They do it for a gold medal that tarnishes and
fades. You're after one that's gold eternally."
(1 Corinthians 9:24–25 MSG)

Just as an athlete follows a schedule that will help him achieve his goal, so too we must begin our spiritual training by following a schedule. Our days are filled with busyness in our fast-paced and constantly connected society. If we do not schedule time for God, our day ends with no thought of Him. Our life then becomes empty, for all the "doings" in life will not lead us to our goal of becoming more like Christ.

However, we begin our journey slowly. We don't run the whole race at once. We train for it a little at a time.

Where do we begin? We need to start simply each morning by speaking to God. We need to thank Him for the beginning of a new day that allows us to start over, again and again, to imitate Him in our words and actions. We need God's help to face the challenges of the day, and we need His strength and guidance through the Holy Spirit to walk faithfully with our loving God. The following prayer sums up our need for prayer with a sense of humour to it:

> *"Dear Lord,*
> *So far I've done all right.*
> *I haven't gossiped,*
> *haven't lost my temper,*
> *and haven't been greedy, grumpy, nasty, selfish,*
> *or overindulgent.*
> *I'm really glad about that.*
> *But in a few minutes, God,*
> *I'm going to get out of bed.*
> *And from then on,*
> *I'm going to need a lot more help.*

— Author unknown

Once morning prayer becomes a habit, we can move on to the next stage. To know God as an intimate friend, we need to read the Bible. The New Testament reveals to us how loving God is and how much He wants to befriend us. Time again is precious, so we will again need to schedule a time where we can be alone with God. Many people I know get up at an earlier time than they usually do to provide this time.

One method of reading Scripture is called Lectio Divina. *Lectio Divina*, a Latin term, means "divine reading" and describes a way of reading the scriptures whereby we gradually let go of our own agenda and open ourselves to what God wants to say to us. You will need to set time aside for this exercise, at least fifteen or twenty minutes each day, and it will be important that you make it a regular practice.

When a person wants to use Lectio Divina as a prayer form, the method is very simple.

1. Make yourself comfortable in a place that is as free from interruptions as possible. Begin with silence for a few minutes, humbly asking God to quiet your heart and make you aware that you are in His loving presence. When you have let go of all your inner distractions, you then can read God's Word with a listening heart and invite God to speak to you through it.

2. Read God's Word (the Gospel for the day) slowly a second time and reflect on what God is saying to you.

3. A word or phrase will become present as God speaks to you. As this passage touches your heart, silently reflect upon it. What is the application to my life? Can I see myself in this scene? What is the specific message? Listen! This type of reflection allows the Holy Spirit to deepen our awareness of God's message.

4. On the third reading of this scripture passage, you need to respond with an open heart. You now courageously speak to Him and tell Him how you will live out His word throughout your day.

If the Word challenges you or raises questions in you, ask God for the grace to understand and live His Word.

5. The last movement of Lectio Divina is to simply rest now in the love that God has for you. Let the words wash over you and ask the Lord how He is inviting you to change. Your prayer here moves beyond words and beyond thought. You simply rest in God. You let God's love transform you.

6. It is a good idea to write down or illustrate the word or phrase that struck you during your reading so you can return to it during the day to remind yourself of the love God has for you and the special message He had for you today.

The next question we need to ask ourselves is, "If you were convicted of being a Christ follower, would there be enough evidence to convict you?" Too many of us are comfortable to go to church on Sunday but fail to live the Gospel at work, at home, in restaurants, etc.

The way to be a convicted Christian is by living and loving so that through us people begin to have a glimpse of the unconditional love that God has shown us in Christ. The best example we can give is to love everyone the way Christ loves: without restriction, without judgment, without condition. If our love for Christ is real, it will lead us to proclaim His message by feeding those who are hungry, by giving shelter to the homeless, by reaching out to the lost and forsaken, and by welcoming the marginalized. Then others, who witness what we do, will "recognize that you are my disciples—when they see the love you have for one another" (John 13:35 MSG)

This means, therefore, that we must push selfish wants out of the way and do what God wants. We must deny ourselves of many things the world considers important, such as happiness, comfort, prosperity, security, friends, good health, fulfilling experiences, and sin. In Paul's letter to the Philippians, we see Christ gives us an example of this:

"Think of yourselves the way Christ Jesus thought of himself. He had equal status with God but didn't think so much of himself that he had to cling to the advantages of that status no matter what. Not at all. When the time came, he set aside the privileges of deity and took on the status of a slave, became human! Having become human, he stayed human. It was an incredibly humbling process. He didn't claim special privileges. Instead, he lived a selfless, obedient life and then died a selfless, obedient death—and the worst kind of death at that—a crucifixion."
(Philippians 2:5-10 MSG)

St. Paul

Christ voluntarily emptied Himself of anything and everything that stood in the way of the glory and gain of His Father through Him.

What about us? Reflecting on your own life, what are some of the things the Lord may be calling on you to sacrifice or give up in order to fulfil His will and purpose or to minister to someone in need?

Will it be easy? No! Sixty years ago, a seventeen-year-old girl left her home to become a nun. She had finished high school and had a job as a teller in a bank. Her parents were not happy with her decision to leave home and enter a convent. Their expectation had been for her to help at home and look after them in their old age. In spite of her parent's disapproval, she entered because she felt sure it is what God was asking her to do. Leaving her parents was one of the hardest things she had to do. One year later, she received her holy habit, but her mother did not come to the ceremony. Her mother finally did visit her and had visited many other sisters in many of our other convents. Sister was then sent on a mission back to Ottawa to become a teacher. Since her parents lived there, she had lots of opportunities to help them out and invited them often to visit and share a meal. On Sister's twenty-fifth anniversary, she asked her mother if she was happy she entered because many of the sisters were very good to her. She answered, "No!" As for Sister, herself, the best decision she ever made was to do what God asked, not do just what would have been easiest.

The Golden Medal of Eternity will be worth all the effort it takes to keep our eyes on God and pray to the Holy Spirit to keep us unselfish enough to follow in His footsteps.

Before going to bed, it is wise and necessary to review the actions and mercies of the day past, so that you may be thankful for all the special mercies and be humble for all our sins. Saint Ignatius of Loyola gave us a simple method called the Daily Examen to help us review each day in a way that will free us to follow God's will. There are four steps to this process.

1. First, we relax in God's presence by thinking of all the love God shows you and all the gifts He has given you. Go over your day and thank God for all the gifts He gave you. Not big things, but little things like, "thanks for saving me from a car accident while

driving," or "thanks for the wonderful friendship of a coworker," or "thanks for the beauty of summer." Thank Him for the gifts you have, such as being able to bring comfort or joy to others.

2. Review your day again, and reflect on how you acted during the day. Ask yourself, where did I meet God today? Look over your experiences of the day and your responses to them. Focus on one or two experiences that stand out. What feelings, urges, reactions, and emotions are associated with the experiences? Did your emotions and reactions bring you closer to God, or move you farther away from Him?

3. Ask for forgiveness. Express sorrow for the times you failed to follow His direction, for hurting others, for not using your own time and gifts well, and ask Him to be with you the next time you meet a similar situation.

4. Ask yourself, what have I learned from this experience? Ask God to help you as you look forward to a new day tomorrow. Promise to cooperate and trust in the loving guidance of the Father, the Son, and the Holy Spirit.

If you make it a habit of doing this Examen daily, you will experience the difference in the way you live. You will grow closer to God in your thoughts, words, and deeds, and will be free to choose to do what He asks you to do.

This approach to prayer will carry you through life, unto death, and on into eternal life.

CHAPTER 14

ETERNAL LIFE

**Within each of us is a bridge drawing us from
earthly life to eternal life with God.**

All that is written on the following pages is from the heart of a believer in God. In a God who created us all to be with Him, all the way, in all truth and with Him forever in a relationship that is everlasting.

Throughout the pages of written and oral history, much has been written on the subject of the question, what follows death? Why is there such a fear of death? Death is as natural as birth! As a society, a people, we tend to focus on all that happens between these two events and seldom do many of us stop to contemplate the hereafter, other than in a whimsical thought process or conversation.

> *"God, as our Creator breathed the 'spirit of life' into us*
> *when with life giving force, He created us! The spirit*
> *in each of us is described as 'the divine breath' which*
> *guarantees the life of every human being and of everything*
> *that exists. To live means to participate in the life of the*
> *life-giving spirit. As long as the spirit is active in a person*
> *he or she lives. But when God withdraws the spirit, life*
> *comes to an end."* [1]

The Kingdom of God goes on to state, "The spirit in human beings is God's Spirit in the sense that God is its Creator." The Spirit's role in all creatures is most explicitly and beautifully expressed in Psalm 104:29–30 ESV:

> *"When you hide your face, they are dismayed;*
> *when you take away their breath,*
> *they die and return to their dust.*
> *When you send forth your Spirit, they are created,*
> *and you renew the face of the ground".*
> *(Psalm 104:29-30 ESV)*

---

1   These words are excerpted from *The Kingdom of God,* written by John Fuellenbach, with originations based on scriptural verses from Genesis.

All of this is to say that God's Spirit is alive and well within us, as long as we yield to that Spirit within us as a life-giving source of grace that fuels our being. Grace is the Spirit of God who descends to the soul of man.

Recently, I attended a meeting where the speaker was Bishop Michael Mulhall, and in reference to eternal life, he said, "We are now experiencing eternal life. Our present lives are a transformation of eternal life." In creating us, God initiated our lives here on earth as phase one, to what is a continuance of an eternal life that culminates in the greatest gift of all—absolute and total peace, joy, and the love of God lavished upon us as we are surrounded by our family and friends.

> *"No one's ever seen or heard anything like this,*
> *Never so much as imagined anything quite like it—*
> *What God has arranged for those who love him."*
> *(1 Corinthians 2:9 MSG)*

Eternal life is now! Our life here on earth is basically a stepping stone or trial period that prepares us for the last leg of our journey, this journey called life.

Within each of us is the Spirit of Christ, which is part of our very being and simply has to be nurtured through the gift of faith.

What is this Spirit of Christ that dwells within us? This Spirit within us is made up of the love and truth that was breathed into us at conception. Each of us is a creation, a formation of God, the Father Almighty. The power of this fact is spelled out in Jesus' own words:

> *"So let me say it again, this truth: It's better for you that I leave. If I don't leave, the Friend won't come. But if I go, I'll send him to you.*
>
> *"When he comes, he'll expose the error of the godless world's view of sin, righteousness, and judgment: He'll show them that their refusal to believe in me is their basic sin; that righteousness comes from above, where I am with the Father, out of their sight and control; that judgment takes*

place as the ruler of this godless world
is brought to trial and convicted."
(John 16: 7–13 MSG)

Let us examine the Wisdom of God! Why would God create a human being with *love* and *truth* as the centrepiece for any other purpose than to spend eternal life with him? At this point, you might ask the question, where does the darkness (sin, doubt, fear, etc.) come from? The answer is that God, in his Wisdom, also granted us free will as part of his masterpiece.

Let us consider the journey of a life in three parts:

1. Life on earth.

2. Death. (The transition that takes place as we move from earthly life to eternal life.)

3. Eternal life.

Taking this into consideration, and knowing that it is part of God's plan, it becomes crystal clear that life on earth has us living out our lives on earth in preparation for eternal life, which is everlasting life with God. Hence, eternal life is *now!*

God is love! God wants us to design our lives around that love using the vehicle of truth that is forever witnessed in

> *The life of Christ,*
> *the lives of the apostles,*
> *the life of our blessed mother,*
> *the lives of the saints,*
> *the prophets,*
> *all truth-sayers.*

Throughout time, these and many more have given their lives over to a passionate way of life that they have faithfully identified as a two-way communication between themselves and God, their Creator.

Deep in thought, in prayer, in meditation, where do we place ourselves? Does the flow of thought within us part company with the external affairs of life, which can tend to dominate and envelop our thought stream? We all have this problem! The focus of our mind needs to begin with an encounter—an encounter with Christ! Is this a chance meeting or a planned summit? Is this relationship one that is building and will continue to grow?

Prayer of this kind takes on a quality of conversation and builds the friendship that becomes a constant relationship with my friend Jesus Christ. It is in this form of mind conditioning that we evaluate the spirit of the W5 (who, where, what, why, and when) of our lives. We remove ourselves from the humdrum of everyday life and move towards the eternal part of our lives, which is not a place but a conditioning of the mind. This is the peace of Christ that will bring us home. With this approach, we will build a bridge from earthly life to eternal life.

In this, the twenty-first century of recorded time here on earth, we continue to question the relevance of eternal life.

Let us begin with our basic working tools:

- Faith and belief system

  We must begin with the Wisdom of God! Our Creator expects us to thrive on all around us, including the arts and sciences that enhance and develop the world we live in. The world we live in, the origins of all the global arts and sciences, have always begun with inspiration. What we fail to realize is that all human inspiration comes from the Wisdom of God. In Faith, God speaks to us constantly through the Holy Spirit.

- Oral history

  Handed down to us over the annals of time are events witnessed and recorded as word of mouth passed on and which have since been substantiated. We have only to research these events and once again we have our reason to draw conclusions.

- Written history

  Some of the first people to share their thoughts, whether in writing on tablets of stone, scrolls, or later on paper, have left us a trail of events that give us our first clues as to the existence and relevance of God. The written message of the Bible has been handed down to us ...

Many people, throughout time, have shared with us their after-life experiences. Having evidenced the valley of death or an out-of-body experience, they tell us about an indescribable, radiant, and alluring light. A source of light that radiates and beacons as a magnet of peaceful acceptance, warmth, and everlasting love. Sometimes that source of light, love, and encouragement comes in an audible form, as it did with my wife, Margaret.

Recently, during a serious illness, Margaret found herself in the intensive care unit of a hospital and fighting a life/death battle. As she hovered in a state of extreme pain, she became aware of a caring, loving voice. She was assured of a state of wellness and urged to continue to look after her husband (me) in the same loving way that God was protecting her.

Whatever these people experienced, we know when they returned to earth, they were changed for the better. These experiences certainly help us to know that there is life after death.

Scripture and tradition teach:

> *"Jesus did not die just to save you from hell.*
> *He paid the price to give you all of heaven."*

— Carlos A. Rodriguez

God loves you and wants you to know Him so He can fill you with peace and give you real life forever. He loves each of us so much that He sent His Only Son to die for you and me. However, we often choose to go our own way and do our own thing rather than choose God's loving way. Sin is choosing to say or do or think things that are against God's plan.

Jesus Christ is God's Son. He is the only one who can bring us back to God. Jesus died on the Cross and rose from the grave. He paid the penalty for our sin and bridged the gap between God and people.

Even though salvation comes from God, we need to respond to the freely given gift of salvation. We need to cooperate with God's saving grace in our lives and thus bring more happiness and fulfilment to our lives in preparation for eternal life.

> *"I tell you a secret, my friend.*
> *Do not wait until the Last Judgment,*
> *It takes place every day."*

— Albert Camus

Each of us will be judged according to the way we have lived our lives here on earth. We will live for love or we will not. We have the freedom to choose between good and evil.

87

As we reflect on eternal life in the present scheme of our existence, the obvious questions arise. What form of preparation are we building as we go forward and live out the continuation of the life that God so lovingly and creatively breathed into us? Are we just being there? Jesus said, "I am the way, I am the truth, and I am the life." With these words, Jesus paints a picture for us to follow. Jesus walks the face of the earth as a human and shows us the way, the truth, and the life that ultimately leads us to a divine life with our Creator. Each of us has been blessed with God-given gifts that our Creator expects us to share with our earthly brothers and sisters as we pass through this very brief part of our journey. As we complete this journey of life, God's wisdom is made available to us.

> *"We don't yet see things clearly. We're squinting in a fog,*
> *peering through a midst. But it won't be long before the*
> *weather clears and the sun shines bright! We'll see it all*
> *then, see it all clearly as God sees us, knowing*
> *Him directly just as He knows us!"*
> *(1 Cor 13:12 MSG)*

Jesus reveals Himself to us, and then later in life, He reveals each of us to ourselves. In teaching us who we really are, God gradually peels away our deficiencies. God carefully creating a desire for more in our on-going awareness of the beauty and majesty that can exist in an intimate relationship with our Creator. It is that relationship that is the central point in our preparation for what can be described as phase two of our eternal life.

> *"Why are you so polite with me, always saying 'Yes, sir,'*
> *and 'That's right, sir,' but never doing a thing I tell you?*
> *These words I speak to you are not mere additions to your*
> *life, homeowner improvements to your standard of living.*
> *They are foundation words, words to build a life on.*
>
> *"If you work the words into your life, you are like a smart*
> *carpenter who dug deep and laid the foundation of his*
> *house on bedrock. When the river burst its banks, and*
> *crashed against the house, nothing could shake it; it was*

built to last. But if you just use my words in Bible studies
and don't work them into your life, you are like a dumb
carpenter who built a house but skipped the foundation.
When the swollen river came crashing in, it collapsed
like a house of cards. It was a total loss."
(Luke 6:46–49 MSG)

In high school, I was taught English literature by Father Brendan Meggannety, who was able to open many literary as well as spiritual doors of my mind during those early years of training. In sharing his gifts with me, a bond was created between us that has remained with me, even though we went our separate ways in short order. Many years later I accidently came across his grave site, realizing he had passed away at sixty-eight years of age. As I gazed upon his memorial stone, it occurred to me that life here on earth is very fleeting and we are given a limited amount of time to apply the gifts that God has so lovingly heaped upon us. Gracious God, let us use the gifts you have given us in keeping with your holy will. It is so important to make it a priority in our earthly lives to establish and maintain a quality relationship with our God, the one that created each one of us. To that end, I share with you the prayer of brother Deacon Lazaro J. Ulloa.

A Deacon's Prayer

Come to my assistance my Lord and my God, that I may
do for You all that you ask.
Strengthen me in adversity and do not let me
succumb to my feelings of worthlessness.
Help me to feel in my heart all that You speak to me,
and help me to understand.
May I be to others what they need:
a body to work with others
when others cannot;
a heart to love those who are forgotten;
a shoulder to console those whose soul is in need;
a smile to brighten the most somber of Your children;

a mouth to proclaim Your Love.
Let me be to You,
as a brush is to a painter,
worthless without You,
but capable of transforming the human heart
by the power of Your mercy.
Send me, my Lord if You need me,
to touch others as You would touch them
as only You can.
Make my heart like Yours,
that I may forgive everything
and love beyond my own human frailty.
Come live within me
that I may die to myself
so You may fill my very being.
Let me serve You.
Do not let me fail, o Lord,
or lead Your people astray.

Allow me to live in your presence today,
that tomorrow I may die in Your hands
and may You raise me one day that I may
touch your face and live in Your glory.

Amen

Imitating His master, Jesus Christ, Maximillian Kolbe demonstrated that he didn't just read the words of scripture in the Bible, but he lived them, to the point of sacrificing his life for them.

At the age of forty-seven years, Father Maximillian Kolbe was put to death in the concentration camp of Auschwitz, where he had been placed for hiding Jews in Poland during Germany's occupation. While in the camp, he offered to take the place of another prisoner who had a family and was chosen to die. The soldier accepted Maximillian's request and threw him down a flight of stairs and left him there with nine other men to starve to death. When it was taking too long for him to die, they threw his weak body into the fire to be burned.

Franciszek Gajowniczek, the man Maximillian replaced, lived another fifty-three years and died when he was ninety-four. Franciszek spent most of his life telling people about the heroic act of love by Maximillian.

Heaven is a place of absolute happiness. Those who go to Heaven are in complete union with God. We call those in Heaven the Communion of Saints. Here, they intercede for us and enjoy perfect communion with the three persons of the Trinity. Heaven is not considered a place, but a personal relationship with God.

As we picture ourselves sitting across from our Creator and consider how we are to be judged, it is essential that we begin by reflecting on Jesus' words, "There is plenty of room for you in my Father's home." (John 14:2 MSG)

As a loving and forgiving God sits across from us, contemplating our earthly lives, pure logic tells us that there are three options. Firstly, the light of Heaven, second, the darkness of Hell." The third option is directly connected with God's mercy. A place (possibly a room?) where we can examine and study our past, a place to take on remorse, a place to consider contrition, and a place where we can reconcile our differences and misdeeds with our God and our fellow man.

In this writer's faith understanding, this place could be called Purgatory. However, if it is not to be named, then suffice to say there is deep meaning in Jesus' own words, "There is plenty of room for you in my Father's home." (John 14:2 MSG)

> "There is plenty of room for you in my Father's home. If that weren't so, would I have told you that I'm on my way to get a room ready for you? And if I'm on my way to get your room ready, I'll come back and get you so you can live where I live. And you already know the road I'm taking."
> (John 14:2–3 MSG)

"But make sure that you don't get so absorbed and exhausted in taking care of all your day-by-day obligations that you lose track of the time and doze off, oblivious to God. The night is about over, dawn is about to break. Be up and awake to what God is doing! God is putting the finishing touches on the salvation work He began when we first believed. We can't afford to waste a minute, must not squander these precious daylight hours in frivolity and indulgence, in sleeping around and dissipation, in bickering and grabbing everything in sight. Get out of bed and get dressed! Don't loiter and linger, waiting until the very last minute. Dress yourselves in Christ, and be up and about! God's kingdom isn't a matter of what you put in your stomach, for goodness' sake."
(Romans 13:11–14 MSG)

Its what God does with your life as He sets it right, puts it together, and completes it with joy. Your task is to single-mindedly serve Christ. Do that and you'll kill two birds with one stone: pleasing the God above you and proving your worth to the people around you."
(Romans 14: 17–18 MSG)

CHAPTER 15

CHALLENGE OF OUR SPIRIT

Our challenge begins with our baptism and continues until we cross the finish line and enter into our eternal kingdom. Jesus sent us the Holy Spirit so that we may be transformed into the image of Christ. Our transformation will depend on how willing we are to allow the Holy Spirit to work in our lives.

> *"Whenever, though, they turn to face God as Moses did, God removes the veil and there they are—face-to-face! They suddenly recognize that God is a living, personal presence, not a piece of chiseled stone. And when God is personally present, a living Spirit, that old, constricting legislation is recognized as obsolete. We're free of it! All of us! Nothing between us and God, our faces shining with the brightness of his face. And so we are transfigured much like the Messiah, our lives gradually becoming brighter and more beautiful as God enters our lives and we become like Him."*
> *(2 Corinthians 3:18 MSG)*

The question now is, "Do you want to take on this challenge?" In other words, do you want only what the world offers or do you want to run towards your heavenly medal that never tarnishes? We can't enter this contest unless we decide to leave aside some of our worldly baggage and begin to train our thoughts on our golden heavenly crown.

To prepare for this challenge, we must value ourselves by understanding that we are special to God because we are His child. Therefore, do not let others convince you to not even begin the challenge. St. Paul tells us that God is enough.

> *"But because God was so gracious,*
> *So very generous, here I am.*
> *And I'm not about to let his grace go to waste."*
> *(1 Corinthians 15:10 MSG)*

We do have a choice? God gave us free will. We choose to love God or to love the world. The fact that God loved us so much that He sent His Son to die to save us from our sins should motivate us to accept this challenge with all our hearts. Winning is not based on speed, intelligence, or wealth. Winning is based on our effort to please God. We win when we do the best we can to please God. Since there will be setbacks, we need the Holy Spirit dwelling within us to help us. He gives us a power that we did not have before. We must allow God's Spirit to operate in our life by submitting to His will. To know His will, we must approach the throne of God in prayer and submission. The Word of God will help us know what God wants us to do.

When we enter this challenge, the course has already been set. We need, however, a coach to train us, so we will know the steps we need to take to accomplish our goal. As Jesus tells us:

> *"I still have many things to tell you, but you can't handle them now. But when the Friend comes, the Spirit of the Truth, He will take you by the hand and guide you into all the truth there is. He won't draw attention to himself, but will make sense out of what is about to happen and, indeed, out of all that I have done and said. He will honor me; he will take from me and deliver it to you. Everything the Father has is also mine. That is*

why I've said, "He takes from me and delivers to you."
(John 16:13–15 MSG)

The Holy Spirit, in a sense then, is our coach on this journey. Like any coach, the Holy Spirit wants us to be the best that we can be. In our prayer, through the reading of scripture, if we listen to Him in the silence of our heart, He will lead us to victory.

Because we are created in God's image and likeness, we are gifted with an unimaginable dignity. This is the ultimate basis of every human being's self-worth and the reason why every person should be respected. The Holy Spirit helps us to realize that the interior self is the person God wants us to be. He teaches us how to use these gifts for others. When we do this, it is then that we begin to become truly human, and in this way, begin to truly reveal Jesus Christ to others:

> *"This resurrection life you received from God is not a timid,*
> *grave-tending life. It's adventurously expectant, greeting*
> *God with a childlike "What's next, Papa?" God's Spirit*
> *touches our spirits and confirms who we really are. We*
> *know who He is, and we know who we are: Father and*
> *children. And we know we are going to get what's coming*
> *to us—an unbelievable inheritance! We go through*
> *exactly what Christ goes through. If we go through the*
> *hard times with him, then we're certainly going to go*
> *through the good times with Him!"*
> *(Romans 8:15–17 MSG)*

"Why did God make you?"

> *"God made you to know Him, to love Him, and to serve*
> *Him in this world, and to be happy with Him*
> *forever in heaven."*
> *(The Baltimore Catechism: Question 6)*

In other words, God made us to become saints. One day, we're going to stand before God, and He's going to say to us, "What did you do with the talents, the abilities, and the background I gave you. How did you use them to build the Kingdom of God in the here and now?

Jesus sent us the gift of the Holy Spirit to guide us to truth. The Holy Spirit consoles us in our trials and assists us as we strive to live out the purpose of our lives. St. Paul tells us, when the Holy Spirit is truly at work in our lives, we will bear much fruit:

> *"...the fruit of the Spirit is love, joy, peace, patience, kindness, generosity, faithfulness, gentleness, and self-control. There is no law against such things.... If we live by the Spirit, let us also be guided by the Spirit."* *(Galatians: 5:22–25 NRSV)*

Each time we act in the name of all that is good *and true, each time we reach out with the love of God that dwells in our hearts to others, the Holy Spirit is at work in our lives.*

Will our journey towards our goal be easy, full of joy, and no pain? We will experience conflicts, pain, problems, or spiritual uneasiness. We should not, however, give up the journey or become bitter and quit the race. Jesus tells us to face the difficulty quickly, and do it face to face. This will help us to grow and mature in character. Suffering is designed to make us better people.

> *"You are full of life now.*
> *Full of passion.*
> *It's how He made you.*
> *Just let it happen."*

> — Anonymous

Nowhere in scripture are we promised that life is going to be easy. In fact, often the opposite is true. Yes, difficulties will come, and trials will cross our paths and often we will be tempted to quit. This means we must give up anything that hinders our relationship with God. We must give up sin and watch our priorities, for they will keep you from finishing the race.

The Holy Spirit gives us the power and the ability to stay away from sin. Paul said, "God did not give us a Spirit of timidity, but a Spirit of power, of love and of self-discipline" (2 Timothy 1:7 NIV)

We should not allow ourselves to be controlled by our old sinful nature, but rather by the Holy Spirit instead. He helps us in our weakness, which gives us the strength to stand firm in the face of temptation.

This challenge is a grueling one, for we will meet long hills to climb and rough patches on the road. Two of these challenges are forgiveness and mercy. Forgiveness is something we all find difficult. God, who is rich in mercy, expects us to imitate Him. In the Gospels, we find Jesus teaching more on forgiveness and mercy than He does on love. If we keep our eyes on Jesus and remember how merciful and forgiving He has been towards us, then we can, through the strength of the Holy Spirit, learn to be like Him. Pope Francis tells us:

> *"Forgiveness is not a result of our efforts, but is a gift. It is a gift of the Holy Spirit who showers us with mercy and grace that pours forth unceasingly from the open heart of Christ crucified and risen."*

Just as a marathoner has to prepare for the race, we too must prepare if we hope to reach our goal—Heaven. We will determine, in this life, where we will spend eternity. If we are going to run the race in the way God intended, we must give it our full attention. To be successful, we must be willing to make sacrifices and lay aside all that deters our walk with God and all that does not make us stronger in the Lord. This race will be won by one who disciplines oneself for the sake of serving Christ, keeping one's body under the control of the Holy Spirit and one's eyes fixed on the goal.

The course is set out for us. We can't make our own course, and if we stray from it, we are disqualified. Some of us are so busy, caught up in everyday life, that we don't even think about eternity or what's really important. Are we caught up in the desire for riches, in the pleasures of the flesh? Are we consumed with work? Are we desperately trying to keep up with the Joneses? Are we filling our life up with more and more materialistic goods and are we finding satisfaction? Are we stuck in the rat race?

Jesus said that if we want to get to Heaven, we have to take the narrow gate. To get through a narrow gate, we can't carry loads of "stuff" with us. If we have bad things in our life—fighting, bad language, disobedience, etc.—we have to let them go. We will never make it into Heaven with sin in our life. We must be willing to take the narrow gate to find God and get rid of whatever we have to in order to see Him. In the end, it's all worth it.

> *"My counsel is this: Live freely, animated and motivated by God's Spirit. Then you won't feed the compulsions of selfishness. For there is a root of sinful self-interest in us that is at odds with a free spirit, just as the free spirit is incompatible with selfishness. These two ways of life are antithetical, so that you cannot live at times one way and at times another way according to how you feel on any given day."*
> *(Galatians 5:16-17 MSG)*

To finish our journey, we will be walking the path of suffering.

> *"I know how great this makes you feel, even though you have to put up with every kind of aggravation in the meantime. Pure gold put in the fire comes out of it proved pure; genuine faith put through this suffering comes out proved genuine. When Jesus wraps this all up, it's your faith, not your gold, that God will have on display as evidence of his victory."*
> *(1 Peter 1:6–7 MSG)*

The path to glory for Christ was the path of unjust suffering. That's our path, also. Our Lord endured suffering with perfect patience and was exalted to the highest point of glory. He is our example of how to respond to suffering. As Christians, we are matured by suffering, identified with Christ, and brought to glory.

No one has ever seen a person who has never trained at the starting line of a marathon race. To enter the race, this person would have to fast from a lot of favourite food in order to be physically fit to run. This also applies to our spiritual journey. St. Paul says:

> "Don't be misled: No one makes a fool of God. What a
> person plants, He will harvest. The person who plants
> selfishness, ignoring the needs of others—ignoring God! —
> harvests a crop of weeds. All he'll have to show for his life is
> weeds! But the one who plants in response to God, letting
> God's Spirit do the growth work in him, harvests a crop
> of real life, eternal life."
> (Galatians 6:7–8 MSG)

If anyone wants to live a life in Christ they must die to self, listen to the guidance of the Holy Spirit, and seek to be holy as God is holy. This will involve giving up sin and give up the things of this world and the evil impulses that emanate from the flesh. We are to let Christ control our actions and thoughts, and let the Holy Spirit be our guide. This requires discipline and effort on our part to make this choice. Each choice we make costs us some of our own selfish will.

Jesus came to us as a little baby, born in poverty, and lived in a very small, poor village. This gives us great hope, for we know He can identify with our plight in life.

God's love for all of us is found in the life of Jesus. During His time on this earth, Jesus associated with every form of humanity, with both saints and sinners. German theologian Helmut Thielicke describes this love with pinpoint perfection as he writes:

> "Jesus gained the power to love harlots, bullies, and ruffi-
> ans. He was able to do this only because He saw through
> the filth and crust of degeneration, because His eye caught

the Divine original which is hidden in every way, in every man. First and foremost, He gives us new eyes. When Jesus loved a guilt-laden person and helped him, He saw in him as an erring child of God. He saw in Him a human being whom His Father loved and grieved over because He was going wrong. He saw him as God originally designed and meant him to be, and therefore He saw through the surface layer of grime and dirt to the real man underneath. Jesus did not identify the person with his sin, but rather saw in this sin something alien, something that really did not belong to him. Something that merely chained and mastered him, and from which He would free him and bring him back to his real self. Jesus was able to love men because He loved them right through the layer of mud."

The Spirit within us is like a channel or pathway that computes the choice or decision we are about to make. We persevere with a single-minded approach and reach a conclusion based on the "staying power" or discipline we have structured our lives to become.

Discipline in a Long-Distance Race

"Do you see what this means—all these pioneers who blazed the way, all these veterans cheering us on? It means we'd better get on with it. Strip down, start running—and never quit! No extra spiritual fat, no parasitic sins. Keep your eyes on Jesus, who both began and finished this race we're in. Study how He did it. Because He never lost sight of where He was headed—that exhilarating finish in and with God—He could put up with anything along the way: Cross, shame, whatever. And now He's there, in the place of honor, right alongside God. When you find, yourselves flagging in your faith, go over that story again, item by item, that long litany of hostility he plowed through. That will shoot adrenaline into your souls!"
Hebrews 12: 1-3 MSG

Will you dare
to live out
this challenge?

CONCLUDING NOTE

We all have individual belief systems.

Whatever your faith or belief system is, know and cherish one fact: we have *all* been created by God; we all start out on an equal footing in the eyes of God.

As a people, we have forgotten who we are!

We have to reclaim our identity. We have to return to the truth of who created us and who we are.

We must return not in fear, but in love.

God wants to reveal Himself to us, but we have to meet God halfway. A suggested starting point might be to look at the love that God has created all around us visually and then listen to the words of love that God has left for us to ponder. Once you have considered these two avenues of approach, you will be well on your way to learning the absolute unwavering love and mercy that God wants to share with each of us.

We simply have to engage.

FURTHER READINGS

Joni: An Unforgettable Story, by Joni Eareckson Tada, Billy Graham, and Joe Musser.

Man's Search for Meaning, by Viktor E. Frankl.

Oscar Romero: Love Must Win Out, by Kevin Clarke.

Reimagining the Ignatian Examen, Mark E. Thibodeaux, SJ.

The Hiding Place, by Corrie ten Boom and Elizabeth Sherrill.

The Kingdom of God, by John Fuellenbach.

The Man Who Got Even with God, by Fr. M. Raymond OSCO.

The Message Bible, Eugene H. Peterson.

The Word Among Us (daily readings + meditations) online @ wau.org

PICTURE REFERENCES

Public Domain Clip Art:

Printed in Canada